Autism B Theory

The Cause, Development and Support of Autism

Stephen Leighton

Clink Street

Published by Clink Street Publishing 2022

Copyright © 2022

First edition.

ISBN: 978-1-915229-06-9 Paperback
978-1-915229-07-6 Ebook

Contents

Introduction

Autism B Theory explains how the autistic brain grows and develops. The theory refers to biology, neuroscience, psychology and lived experience to explain the wider phenomena associated with the autistic spectrum.

It is constantly highlighted throughout the book that there is no cure for autism. It is hoped that Autism B Theory can finally end the narrative of eugenics, ensuring future research is focused on providing better support and understanding.

Most books about autism are either written for non-autistic people to understand autism, or for autistic people to understand themselves better. This book is trying to break that mould, as any autism theory should explain the brain development of both autistic and non-autistic people.

Some of the topics covered are complex areas of brain development so they have been written in a way to ensure the lay person can understand.

Chapter 1 gives a brief overview of autism.

Chapter 2 explains Autism B Theory.

Chapter 3 explains why pregnancies are biologically demanding.

Chapter 4 explains why there is a higher prevalence of autistic people conceived in winter months.

Chapter 5 explains the biochemical pathways involved with autism.

Chapter 6, 7 and 8 explain how sensory sensitivities can develop through atypical myelination of sensory and motor neurons which impacts on sensitive and critical periods of development.

Chapter 9 explains how social communication skills develop.

Chapter 10 explains emotional development.

Chapter 11 explains why some areas of social development can be difficult for autistic people.

Chapter 12 explains how executive function skills can be difficult for autistic people.

Chapter 13 describes autistic attention.

Chapter 14 explains why autistic people often experience poor mental health.

Chapter 15 explains why autistic people often experience trauma.

Appendix 1 highlights some support autistic people may find useful for themselves.

Appendix 2 highlights some practical support non-autistic people can help support autistic people with.

Chapter 1
What is autism?

Autism is a neurodevelopmental disposition.

- Neuro: meaning brain.
- Developmental: refers to how the brain grows and develops.
- Disposition: a person's inherent qualities of mind and character.

This means that each autistic person will have a different connected brain from the majority of society, however, each autistic person will have their own unique way of perceiving and interacting with the world; this is why it is called a spectrum.

There are many terms that people use when talking about autism. Some of these are autistic, someone with autism, Asperger's, aspie, auty, infantile autism, high functioning autism, autism spectrum disorder, on the spectrum, neurodiversity and neurodivergence. Each autistic person will have their own preference for terminology.

People often refer to autism as neurodiversity. However, neurodiversity covers the full range of all brain diversity which includes both autistic and non-autistic people. Therefore, strictly speaking, neurodiversity doesn't exclusively mean autism. Instead, some autistic people prefer neurodivergence or neurodivergent. Neurodivergence doesn't mean good or bad, it just means different compared with the brains of the majority of society.

As brain development of non-autistic people is more or less the same they're often referred to as neurotypical people. The term neurotypical will now be used throughout this book to describe non-autistic people.

You may have heard of the term atypical development in relation to autism. This is because the autistic brain grows and develops differently compared to neurotypical people, hence their development will be atypical.

Neurodivergence also refers to many other neuro-differences, such as:

- ADHD: difficulty with focus, attention, and planning.
- Dyslexia: difficulty learning to read, interpreting words, letters and other symbols.
- Dyscalculia: difficulty processing numbers.
- Hyperlexia: reading ability much earlier than expected.
- Dyspraxia: difficulty in activities requiring coordination and movement.

As neurodivergence can mean many things, the terms autism and autistic will now be used throughout this book.

Autism will mean different opportunities, strengths, and difficulties for each person which can cause confusion for people when trying to initially understand autism. This is because autism often manifests differently in so many people. For example, how can a two-year old, a teenager, a woman with a family, an adult with an intellectual disability and a man working fulltime all be autistic but still be so different? Hopefully this book provides clarity for such questions.

There is no simple way to diagnose autism. The process of diagnosis will look at a detailed history of the person, identifying if they have always had experiences, strengths and challenges associated with the autistic spectrum. Loosely speaking, if there is history of autistic behaviour and experiences from childhood, and throughout their life, a diagnosis of autism will likely be made. Generally speaking, the diagnostic process will look at experiences, strengths and challenges within the following four domains:

- Communicating.
- Social and emotional understanding.
- Planning and organising (flexible thinking and executive functioning).
- Sensory sensitivities.

It is generally considered that autism cannot be diagnosed before the age of two. This is because there needs to be enough time before any difference can be observed with developmental milestones in relation to sensory motor coordination, communication, social skills and problem-solving ability.

Many autistic children reach milestones early or on time but show signs of atypical development in later stages. Some autistic children may reach developmental milestones late or not at all.

Generally, autistic babies between birth and six months are less likely to look, smile or make sounds to people. From six to twelve months autistic babies are more likely to look, smile and talk to objects rather than people. At times they may show an increased reaction to people, however, this still remains at a lower level when compared to typical development.

It is often in the second year of life when language, communication and play become noticeably different in autistic children. This is when parents notice differences with speech and language, indifference to others and difficulty with change. They may also notice that their child's play is different. For some children, parents may report incredible skills or islets of ability beyond their age and stage in relation to reading, speaking and naming things.

Between twelve and twenty-four months some autistic children may show little response to what is said to them (known as a difficulty with receptive language), and may only use a few words in a meaningful way (known as difficulty with expressive language). Another example of poor reciprocity is difficulty taking turns in conversation. Some children may exhibit echolalia (repeating what has been said to them or repeating well-rehearsed phrases).

Between the age of two and three-years autistic children may show little eye contact or joint attention. Some may also have difficulty with protodeclarative pointing (pointing to indicate or share with others their interest in something). Some parents report their autistic child seemed to be developing perfectly normally, until at some point, (usually around the second year), their development seemed to stagnate or regress.

Between the age of three and five years autistic children may prefer playing on their own, being more occupied with things rather than people.

The brain will have developed 50% by the first six months, and 80% by the first eighteen months of life. The development of the brain within the first 18 months is the foundation that all future learning is built upon. This highlights how crucial sensitive and critical periods of development are.

A sensitive period is a limited time window which the effects of experience influence neural and physical development.

A critical period is defined as an exact time window for specific neural and physical development to take place. If a learning opportunity is missed during a critical period, then the young person may never be able to learn that skill.

As the autistic brain develops atypical, it may meet some milestones early, or sometimes not at all. This will likely result in some strengths and some challenges for the autistic person. Everyone will be different but there are common themes of being autistic. This is why Figure 1 can help people initially understand the range of the autistic spectrum experiences and challenges.

Some autistic people may have special islets of ability, some may have an exceptional high IQ, some may even have savant abilities and other autistic people may need intense support.

For example, if a child has not developed the social skills needed by the age of five years, then it appears they have lost the critical period to unconsciously learn the social rules of reciprocity, flexibility and cooperation needed for social interactions. Such atypical development can explain why autistic people may have social communication challenges throughout their life.

School, college, work, day care, daily life and relationships can all be fraught with difficulty if not properly planned or supported. This often leads to burnout, fatigue, and breakdown for autistic people across the whole spectrum. This makes autistic people vulnerable to poor mental health by being constantly exposed to potential traumatic experiences.

You can see a more detailed description of some of the strengths and challenges experienced by autistic people in Figure 1. Every person will be different, but to be diagnosed autistic the person will have at least have some strengths and challenges in each of the four domains. It starts to become clear how challenges in one domain can cause difficulty within another.

For example, an autistic child may have struggled at nursery with joint attention and play (communication and social). Then, at school the same person may have had difficulty maintaining a two-way conversation (communication) and struggled with overhead fluorescent lights (sensory). Then as the person progressed to work they may have had difficulty understanding the intentions of others (social), as well as the planning needed for the constant changes of work practices (executive function skills and attention). Then when the person has their own home they struggle to prioritise housework and sort mail (executive function skills and attention) As you can see, autism has always been there, it just presents itself differently throughout a person's life.

Figure 1: autism reflection box.

Communicating	Social and emotional understanding	Executive function skills and attention	Sensory sensitivities
Non-speech communication, body language, eye-gaze, body positioning.	Empathy, seeing others point of view.	Organisation.	Sensory seeker (hypersensitive). sensory avoider (hyposensitive).
Receptive communication, whether this is using specific objects, generalised objects, gestures, photographs, drawing, formal signs – such as Makaton, symbols, speech or written language.	Understanding social norms, such as reciprocity, unwritten rules, manners, humour.	Attention, focus and special interests.	Differences in processing sounds/ noises.

Communicating	Social and emotional understanding	Executive function skills and attention	Sensory sensitivities
Expressive communication, whether this is using specific objects, generalised objects, gestures, photographs, drawing, formal signs – such as BSL/Makaton, symbols, speech or written language.	Understanding social situations, such as different roles, expectations or norms. Insensitive/indifferent to others.	Motivation.	Differences in processing proprioception inputs such as body awareness.
Echolalia: repeating specific noises, words or catchphrases which appear to have no significant meaning.	Social use of language. For example, what to say, who to say it to, Where and when to say it, Questions – too many/too few.	Planning/initiative.	Differences in processing vestibular inputs such as balance and movement.
Communicating feelings and emotions.	Poor joint attention. Lack of interaction/interest in others.	Working memory.	Differences in processing visual inputs/filtering.
Communicating likes, preferences or choices.	Understanding/respecting personal space.	Generalising/understanding the wider context.	Differences in processing smells.
Communicating dislikes/unhappiness.	Difficulty with relationships, either establishing or maintaining.	Problem-solving/learning new skills.	Differences in processing tastes.
Communicating difficulties.	Understanding own emotions, and/or the emotions of others.	Predicting what will happen next, Outcomes/consequences of actions.	Differences in processing touch.
Starting/ending a communication effectively and/or appropriately. Developing two-way communication.	Over/underestimated emotional responses.	Understanding the context of situations/events.	Differences in pain tolerances.
Talking too much/too little.	Understanding motive/intent of others.	Difficulty with big/small changes and/or transitions.	Difficulty in regulating temperature/thirst/hunger.
Situational mutism.	Difficulty offering/asking for help.	Concept of time/time management.	Differences in reactions to thirst/hunger.

Communicating	Social and emotional understanding	Executive function skills and attention	Sensory sensitivities
Engaging in reciprocal turn taking when communicating.	Inappropriate social behaviours, such as sharing too much information or too honest.	Decision making.	Distress towards physical changes in environment.

To help develop a deeper understanding of autism this book will explore all the associated phenomena of the autistic disposition.

Chapter 2
What is Autism B Theory?

This chapter gives a detailed overview of Autism B Theory. Each chapter that follows will focus on certain aspects of the theory to help develop a deeper understanding of how the autistic brain grows and develops.

It is generally accepted that autism is now as common as one person in fifty in the population, with some research claiming it is even higher. When all the known causes (highlighted below) are collated, they don't account for the steadily increasing autistic prevalence rates. Also, there are still some people who are born autistic without any of the known causes present, this obviously means there has to be something naturally causing autism.

Here are some of the traditional known associated causes of autism:

- Hereditary genetics.
- Difficult births.
- Mitochondria disease.
- Cranial folate deficiency.
- CT776 gene variations.
- Exposure to toxins and toxic metal.
- Pernicious anaemia (PA).
- Auto immune difficulties and poor microbiome (gut health).
- Genetic mutations and various others.

Autism B Theory

Autism B Theory explains the biological surge during pregnancy will inevitably mean some babies will be at risk of being deficient in either vitamin B6 (pyridoxine), B9 (folate) and B12 (cobalamin), or a deficiency combination of all three. Such deficiency can impact baby development within a number of biochemical pathways which could help explain both the natural cause of autism and the increasing prevalence rates observed across the world.

Vitamin B6, B9 and B12 are essential for overall health and brain function. They are essential because the body cannot make these vitamins on its own, it can only get them from nutrition. Research highlights that 19-29% of pregnant mothers are vitamin B deficient (particularly B12) during, and, or straight after pregnancy [1, 2]. This included mothers who had a rich diet, as well as mothers who had a rich diet including vitamin supplements. This therefore highlights that such deficiencies are not a result of poor dietary or lifestyle choices by the mother, instead the deficiency just seems to be a natural occurring biological demand during pregnancy. Again, for clarity, the deficiency is not the mother's fault.

A mother with lower levels of B vitamins as a result of the biological demand during and just after pregnancy may also result in the baby being low in vitamin B, particularly B12. Even after birth the baby is still dependent on absorbing vitamin B6, B9 and B12 from the mother through breastfeeding. It takes a period of time (days, weeks and maybe months) for the vitamin B levels of some women to return to normal levels after pregnancy. This will naturally mean some babies may also be vitamin B deficient for some periods of time.

Low levels in some of the B vitamins (B6, B9 and B12, or in a combination of all three) may result in atypical differences within certain biochemical pathways needed for overall health and early development. Interestingly, all the already known causes of autism are also involved in the same biochemical pathways that are dependent on these three B vitamins. The biochemical pathways are discussed in more detail in chapter 5.

Autism B theory hypotheses difficulty with these pathways, specifically the atypical myelination patterns of neurons as a result of lower levels of B vitamins, could be the precursor for developing the autistic disposition.

Figure 2 is an overview of Autism B Theory.

Traditional associated causes of autism

Hereditary genetics   Mitochondria disease
Cranial folate and Vitamin D deficiency Poor microbiome (gut health)
CT776 gene variations   Exposure to toxins/toxic metal
Pernicious Anaemia (PA)   Auto immune difficulties
Genetic mutations and various others

Autism B Theory

The biological demand of pregnancy means 19-29% of pregnant mothers are vitamin B deficient, therefore influencing the atypical development of biochemical pathways for baby development highlighted below. This could explain the natural cause of autism. These are the same biochemical pathways involved with the traditional associated causes of autism.

Biochemical pathways involved with autism

The folate cycle. Folate (vitamin B9) is important in red blood cell formation, healthy cell growth and function. Folate is crucial during early pregnancy as it is required for helping other essential biochemical pathways such as epigenetics and methylation processes.

Pyrimidine and purine synthesis. Both provide the building blocks for DNA and RNA. Purines provide the necessary energy and cofactors to promote cell survival and reproduction.

Methionine processes. Methionine is an antioxidant. It helps detoxify harmful substances in the body such as heavy metals.

Methylation. Methylation is an epigenetic mechanism used by cells to control gene expression. It helps turn on and off the right genes at the right time.

Homocysteine regulation. Homocysteine is an amino acid. Vitamins B6, B9 and B12 help break down homocysteine to create other chemicals the body needs. High homocysteine levels are often a consequence of a vitamin B deficiency, often resulting in poor autoimmune health and pain associated difficulties.

Glutathione. Glutathione is involved in tissue building and repair. It also supports making chemicals and proteins that the body needs for a healthy immune system.

Regulation of methylmalonic acid. B12 is used in the regulation of methylmalonic acid (MMA). Too much MMA can result in neuropathy, including a breakdown of the cell wall and poor myelination of developing neurons during early baby development.

Sensory motor stage 0-2 years

Atypical development of the biochemical pathways will likely result in sensory sensitivity. Atypical myelination of neurons can develop a atypical sensory motor system which will result in sensory sensitivities. There will also potentially be atypically myelinated neurons of the Social Engagement System which will contribute to atypical social development.

Emotional stage of development (2-3 years)

An atypical embodied sense of self will subsequently result in atypical emotional development.

Social development (3-5 years)
Different myelinated Social Engagement System neurons, and atypical emotional regulation will mean the young person will unlikely learn the unconscious social skills social fluidity, reciprocity and capacity to deal with change within critical periods of development.
Lifelong atypical development and neurodivergence
The autistic person will struggle to socially connect, engage or problem solve in the dominant neurotypical world. If not supported, the person may be vulnerable to poor mental health, isolation, trauma and poor life outcomes.

Low levels of vitamin B at key stages of early development may increase the chances of developing an autistic disposition naturally. Nevertheless, it is conceivable that pregnant mothers who are exposed to the traditional associated causes of autism may mean the child is more prone to developing an autistic disposition.

Low levels of B vitamins will likely impact on the myelination of some of the first developing neurons. Autism B theory predicts that future research will continue to link the cause of autism with atypical myelination of neurons [3,4].

Figure 3: A neuron.

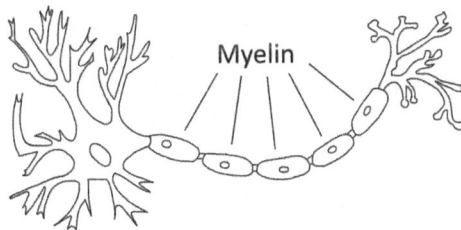

Myelin is a white fatty substance that wraps around the axon of a neuron like a sheath. Myelin insulates the axons of most neurons, helping speed up communication between neighbouring neurons. For example, more myelination results in faster communication and less myelination means slower communication.

If there are low levels of vitamin B during a baby's development (even during pregnancy), this could result in atypical myelination for the very first neurons of the developing brain and wider nervous system. Even a short period of low vitamin B may result in neuro-developmental differences. As early as the second trimester of pregnancy, neuronal connections are made at an incredible rate. The brain goes through the biggest neuronal growth in the first six months of life. For example, over one million neuron connections are made every second.

Some of the very first neurons to be myelinated are motor and social engagement neurons. It makes sense to myelinate these neurons first as they help the baby move and socially communicate. Interestingly, these two sets of neuron pools are central to autism. For example, atypical myelination of motor neurons can lead to sensory sensitivities, and atypical myelination of social engagement neurons can lead to social communication differences. Also, sensory sensitivities and social communication differences will likely result in atypical executive functioning skills.

As already explained, Autism B Theory hypothesises low levels of B vitamins during early development is likely to be the explanation for the natural development of autism. However, any unified theory also has to explain the associated phenomena with autism such as:

- Sensory sensitivities (hyper/hypo) with sight, hearing, taste, tactile difficulties and hypo proprioceptive needs.
- Difference with elements of communication.
- Difference with elements of social interaction.
- Difference with elements of executive functioning skills.
- Potential difficulty with sarcasm and grey areas of conversation.
- Difficulty with change, especially unexpected change (big or small).
- Difficulty with perceived demands.
- Attention, fixed interests and repetitive movements.
- Potential extra cranial size in early childhood.
- Higher prevalence of epilepsy.
- Higher prevalence of gut and autoimmune issues.
- Higher prevalence of LGBTQ disposition.
- Slighter higher prevalence with C-section birth.
- More autistic people conceived in winter months.

14

- High degree of genetic heritability.
- That no two autistic brains are the same.

Autism B theory explains all the above phenomena.

The biological surge of pregnancy for some women (19-29%) has always likely resulted in autism, but this doesn't explain why there is a steady increase in prevalence rates. Better awareness may have contributed to some increase in prevalence rates, however, Autism B theory hypothesises the overreliance of processed foods in modern society (packaged foods, tins, bottles and foods with unusually long shelf lives) may play some role in the increased rates of autism. Adequate gut health (the microbiome) helps break down foods to absorb the essential nutrients it needs for health. Processed foods decrease the functioning of good gut health, eventually negatively impacting on the gut to absorb key nutrients such as B vitamins. Gut health is discussed in more detail in Appendix 7.

The human gut has a ratio of both good and opportunistic bacteria. The ratio is for every eight good bacteria there are two opportunistic bacteria. Basically, the good and opportunistic bacteria work together. The good bacteria help the body absorb the good nutrition and the opportunistic bacteria is good at killing off pathogens and harmful bacteria. This is why the ratio of 8:2 helps keep the gut healthy.

The modern diet is reliant on foods and nutrition that has a long shelf life (tins, bottles, cans and packages). The reason why these foods have a long shelf life is because these foods have been coated with bacteria-killing properties in order to keep the food or liquid from decomposing. When people eat processed foods they are also digesting the bacteria-killing properties that are used to coat the food to ensure a longer shelf life, this can affect the healthy bacteria ratio of 8:2 in the gut. Such absorption therefore negatively impacts the guts ability to break down foods, absorb nutrition and fight off infection.

As some women (19-29%) will be deficient in B vitamins during pregnancy (through no fault of their own), then anything that affects their gut health ratio may further impact on their ability to absorb B vitamins (particularly

B12). This may also mean they are more vulnerable to the traditional known causes of autism. Could it be the that the modern diet is slightly putting more stress on the microbiome of pregnant mothers who are already deficient in B vitamins (through no fault of their own) that is contributing to the increased prevalent rates of autism?

Autism B Theory can also explain why there is an increase of autistic people being conceived in winter months, and why there is a higher chance of a baby being autistic if delivered by C-section.

The body needs vitamin D to absorb vitamin B12 in the gut. Humans get about 80% of vitamin D through natural sunlight. The lack of vitamin D during the winter months may impact on the gut's ability to absorb vitamin B12 from nutrition. If the gut cannot get enough vitamin D it will then have difficulty absorbing B12 from nutrition. This coupled with low levels of B vitamins due to the biological demand of pregnancy may help explain why there are more autistic people conceived in winter months.

This can also help explain why some babies delivered by C-section have an increased chance of being autistic. If a baby is delivered by C-section it loses the opportunity to be covered with vaginal fluid during birth. The vaginal fluid helps kickstart the baby's autoimmune system (gut health). Without the opportunity to acclimatise to unknown pathogens, the baby's gut is at a disadvantage and may therefore develop poor autoimmune and gut related difficulties during early development and later life. This may result in a difficulty in absorbing vitamin B during early development, especially if the mother has lower levels of B vitamins.

All three B vitamins (B6, B9 and B12) play a crucial role in the many biochemical pathways for health and development, but they also play a significant role with the regulation of MMA (methylmalonic acid). B12 is needed to regulate MMA. Too much MMA may result in neuropathy and atypical myelination patterns of some of the first developing neurons during baby development, particularly the motor neurons that help develop voluntary control of limbs and muscles.

Atypical myelination (especially sensory motor neurons) will mean that information will be slowly, or poorly, communicated between the brain, body and wider nervous system. This will obviously result in sensory integration difficulties.

Research is starting to highlight that an autism diagnosis in relation to motor movement for babies is becoming possible. What these diagnostic assessments will highlight is the baby's lack of voluntary movement within the first year of life. The lack of voluntary motor movement will be measured by various things such as eye movement, head turns, limb movement, and movement to noise to determine if a baby will likely develop an autistic disposition [5].

Most autistic people (if not all) will have sensory sensitivities. This is usually sensitive to certain lights, noises, textures, feelings on the skin, sensitive to certain tastes and profound proclivity for stimming (self-stimulating behaviours such as repetitive movements). Stimming is essentially the process of activating sensory motor movement.

Autistic people are usually over or under sensitive within their sensory preferences. However, the sense of proprioception (the sense of the position of body in space) is the only sense that autistic people are usually under sensitive with.

Autistic people enjoy stimming. This is because the movement stimulates proprioceptive sensors located throughout the body's muscles and tendons. For example, many autistic people really enjoy rocking, head movements, finger flicking, toe-tapping, tiptoe walking, swinging, trampolining and deep pressure stimulation. This stimming behaviour helps the brain have a frame of reference of where the muscles are, helping the brain plan for potential voluntary movement. The proprioception neurons are some of the first neurons to be myelinated.

Children have to integrate their awareness of their body parts (proprioception) with all their other senses. This is because the proprioception system works with all the sensory systems to help the brain integrate all the sensory information (sensory integration). Around 70% of the information that is sent to the brain is done so through motor pathways (supported by proprioceptor receptors in the muscles) [6]. The receptors inform the brain where the body parts are. This helps the brain integrate all the other senses with the body so it can understand what is being perceived. For example, to look you need to use muscles to turn your head and eyes. To listen you need to turn your head and flex tiny ear muscles to distinguish certain noise, tones and pitch. To talk and eat you need to flex muscles within the mouth. To understand what is on the palm of your hand (skin) you need muscle movement to feel. This is why 70% of sensory information that is sent to the brain is done so through motor pathways as it helps the brain fully integrate all sensory experiences.

The motor neurons that are atypically myelinated during early development will impact on the baby's ability for voluntary control within the first two years of life. This can explain why there is continued research to develop a sensory moving assessment for babies to determine if they are autistic [5]. As the brain is already wired 80% by the first eighteen months, it is likely that the development of the autistic brain is closely related to sensory motor movement.

Every autistic brain will be different, and this can explain why different people will have different sensory sensitivities. Below is an explanation to help understand how such sensory differences can unfold, especially during the first eighteen months of life when one million neuron connections are being made every second.

Oversensitive to sensory stimulation within the first eighteen months

Sight sensitivity. If the head and eyes cannot move quickly enough, then light will burn the retina which will eventually result in extra sensitivity.

Smell sensitivity. If the head and nostrils cannot move quickly to avoid strong smells, then in time the brain may become oversensitive to certain smells.

Hearing sensitivity. If the head cannot move quickly enough to distinguish certain noises, the brain may have difficulty knowing where the noise is coming from. This may result in the brain becoming oversensitive to certain noises. Also, if the motor neurons in the ear (the third ear muscle) are not sending information to the brain quick enough, it can be hard for the brain to distinguish certain tones and pitch. This may result in difficulty hearing or expressing tone, pitch and emotion within communication (monotone robotic speech).

Taste sensitivity. Taste receptors in the mouth will taste things, however, the brains ability to understand texture is needed by muscle movement. The information from the texture receptors may not reach the brain quickly enough, therefore the brain may become oversensitive to anything entering the mouth as choking is an obvious danger to life. This might explain why autistic people may develop restricted diets and preferences for certain foods and textures.

Tactile (skin) sensitivity. Receptors detect all things the skin comes into contact with. The receptors are trying to determine primary qualities such as hot, cold, smooth, soft, sharp and rough. The information from these receptors also requires motor movement to help distinguish other primary qualities for things such as size. If the motor neurons can't send the information to the brain quick enough, the brain may become oversensitive with tactile sensation. This helps explain why some autistic people may become oversensitive to temperatures, clothes, socks and so on.

Under sensitive to sensory stimulus within the first eighteen months

The only sense that an autistic person is usually not over sensitised with is proprioception. Most autistic people (if not all) have poor proprioceptive awareness.

Proprioception is the brains ability to sense movement, action, and location of body parts. Proprioception receptors are located in the muscles and tendons throughout the body. When these receptors are activated it helps the brain understand what the body is doing. For example, you could be blindfolded and sit on a chair. Although you can't see the chair, the proprioception receptors inform your brain what you are doing.

The proprioception sense works closely with the vestibular system. The vestibular system is the sense of balance which stops someone from falling over. It is also needed to help people locate things in their field of vision as well as sounds in the environment.

The vestibular system is located in the inner ear. The vestibular system consists of fluid in the ear canals. As the person moves so does the fluid. The movement of the fluid, combined with the pressure felt by the proprioceptor receptors throughout the body informs the brain how and where the body is moving. The proprioception and vestibular system makes up the sensory motor system. If there are atypically myelinated proprioceptor neurons, then this will likely result in under sensitivity for some autistic people in relation to balance, vision and hearing. Again, this helps explain why some autistic people may need to stim, as the stimming helps the brain better integrate other sensory experiences.

Slower proprioception pathways (as a result of atypically myelinated neurons) may mean the brain is not able to fully integrate what is being perceived, therefore, the brain may demand the person seek out even more of that sensory stimulus as this helps the brain have more sensory stimulation to help understand things in the environment better. This can help explain why some autistic people may seek additional sensory preferences around some senses but avoid others.

An under-responsive sensory motor system will often mean different things for different people. For example, some people may experience difficulties with fragmented perception, delayed sensory processing, clumsiness, poor coordination, poor fine motor and gross motor skills, tiptoe walking, hand flapping, a love of swings and trampolines, a love of stimming behaviours, enjoy fidget toys, finger flicking, toe tapping, needing to touch things in the environment (this helps the body have a reference point), and often bending limbs when sitting.

The other set of motor neurons to be myelinated during early development are the ones needed to start developing social skills. These neurons help develop parts of the Social Engagement System which is responsible for screening faces, imitation and expressing emotion over the face (discussed in more detail in chapter 9). Atypical myelination of these social neurons will likely result in atypical social development.

Atypically myelinated mirror neurons may also impact on the baby's ability to imitate others in the environment.

Atypically myelinated neurons will mean autistic children will develop atypically. This will mean they will not meet sensitive and critical periods of development the way neurotypical people do.

The brain is dependent on the body, and the body is dependent on motor neurons to act in the world. Even simple tasks such as walking, talking, eating and communicating are all outputs of myelinated motor neurons. Even to think about doing something involves the brain using motor neurons to plan potential actions. Such skills are described as executive functioning (discussed in more detail in chapter 12). Figure 4 highlights how sensory motor integration is needed for overall daily life and cognition.

Figure 4: Sensory motor integration needed for action and cognition.

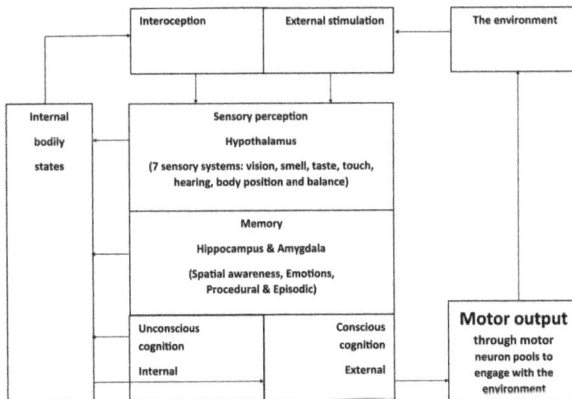

Autism B Theory summary

Autism B Theory explains low levels of B vitamins during and after pregnancy can explain what may naturally cause autism. Such natural occurring low levels of B vitamins are nobody's fault. It could even be argued that such low levels is nature's way of ensuing diversity. Humanity has greatly benefited from such diversity and this book is trying to promote the idea that autistic people should be celebrated and fully supported.

The following chapters start to build on the basic introductions made in this chapter, eventually explaining autism in more detail.

References

1. Prevalence of vitamin B-12 insufficiency during pregnancy and its effect on offspring birth weight: a systematic review and meta-analysis. Author: Sukumar, Nithya; Rafnsson, Snorri B. Publication: The American Journal of Clinical Nutrition. Publisher: Oxford University Press. Date: 2016-04-13

2. Ries, Julia. "Pregnant Women Aren't Getting Enough Nutrients." Healthline, Healthline Media, 24 June 2019, https://www.healthline.com/health-news/pregnant-women-arent-getting-the-vitamins-and-nutrients-they-need?msclkid=91a49710c15b11ec9fdf312770d44b13.

3. Deoni, S., Zinkstok, J., Daly, E., Ecker, C., Williams, S., & Murphy, D. (2015). White-matter relaxation time and myelin water fraction differences in young adults with autism. Psychological Medicine, 45(4), 795-805. doi:10.1017/S0033291714001858

4. Basilis Zikopoulos, Xuefeng Liu, Justin Tepe, Iris Trutzer, Yohan J John, Helen Barbas. 2018. "Opposite development of short- and long-range anterior cingulate pathways in autism." ACTA NEUROPATHOLOGICA, Volume 136, Issue 5, pp. 759 – 778. https://doi.org/10.1007/s00401-018-1904-1).

5. Torres, E. and Whyatt, C., 2018. Autism: The movement-sensing perspective. 1st ed. Boca Raton : CRC Press, Taylor & Francis Group, [2018].

6. David, Alfred. The Secret Life of the Brain: Unlocking the Mysteries of the Mind, Cassell, London, 2019, p. 99.

Chapter 3

Pregnancy, vitamin B and why all humans are born premature

Human babies are born premature when compared to other mammals. For example, a deer is upright and running within hours of birth, but it takes a human baby two years to master similar sensory motor development [1,2]. The gestation period (in the womb) should be between eighteen and twenty-one months for humans when compared to other mammals, but somehow it is only nine months. There are three possible explanations why.

1. Large human brain size and upright locomotion.
2. Potential metabolic demand of a pregnancy supporting a large brain.
3. Extra development outside the womb to maximise cognitive and social development.

Large brain size and upright locomotion

The evolution of humans walking upright (bipedalism) has restricted the potential for an increased width of the birth canal. This makes nine months the optimal time a baby can be in the womb before they become too big to pass through. The brain continues to develop outside of the womb, nearly doubling in size during the first year of life.

Potential metabolic demand of a pregnancy supporting a large brain.

Another explanation is the potential metabolic demand placed on the mother when supporting the baby's growth in the womb, specifically the baby's brain and nervous system. Once outside of the womb, the baby's growth slows down to a more sustainable rate [3]. The biological demand can explain why 19-29% of pregnant mothers are deficient in B vitamins [4,5].

Data from a wide range of mammals suggests that the explosive growth of a foetus during pregnancy places significant biological demand on the mother. By nine months the metabolic demands of the baby threaten to exceed the mother's ability to meet both the baby's energy requirements as well as her own. Therefore, from a biological perspective it seems that nine months is the optimal time a baby can stay in the womb. This is sometimes referred to as the metabolic crossover hypothesis [6].

Extra development outside the womb to maximise cognitive and social development.

Babies will learn cognitive and social skills much quicker outside of the womb as the largest growth period of brain development happens within the first 18 months of life.

A baby is born with 100 billion neurons, this is significantly more than adults. The extra neurons help babies learn quickly, ensuring all learning is done within sensitive and critical periods of development.

The extra neurons communicate and eventually connect with other neurons throughout the brain and nervous system. These connections form synapses, and these synapses become more sophisticated as the baby grows and develops. Eventually these synapses become neuro-networks, helping the baby learn and grow, developing cognitive and social skills.

One of the main processes which help the baby's brain develop is the myelination of neurons in the brain and wider nervous system. A baby's brain will start myelinating neurons around thirty-two weeks into pregnancy. Myelination helps support brain growth development, enabling the brain to grow in size which naturally puts additional demand on the metabolic capacity of mother during the pregnancy and subsequent breastfeeding.

Figure 5: Neuron network.

All three explanations of why babies are born premature when compared to other mammals are helpful. However, the metabolic demand during pregnancy can help explain why 19-29% of women are vitamin B deficient during and after pregnancy [7].

Not every pregnancy which is low in vitamin B will result in autism, but the research of metabolic demand on pregnancy can explain why a small percentage of this group (19-29%) may have atypical biochemical pathways which could explain the natural cause for autism.

References

1. Carr, Alan. The Handbook of Child and Adolescent Clinical Psychology: A Contextual Approach. Routledge, 2013.
2. Martin RD. Primate Origins and Evolution: A Phylogenetic Reconstruction. Princeton, New Jersey: Princeton Univ Press; 1990. [Google Scholar]).
3. Wong, Kate. "Why Humans Give Birth to Helpless Babies." Scientific American Blog Network, Scientific American, 28 Aug. 2012, https://blogs.scientificamerican.com/observations/why-humans-give-birth-to-helpless-babies/. All mammals metabolic burden during pregnancy.

4. Prevalence of vitamin B-12 insufficiency during pregnancy and its effect on offspring birth weight: a systematic review and meta-analysis. Author: Sukumar, Nithya; Rafnsson, Snorri B. Publication: The American Journal of Clinical Nutrition. Publisher: Oxford University Press. Date: 2016-04-13

5. Ries, Julia. "Pregnant Women Aren't Getting Enough Nutrients." Healthline, Healthline Media, 24 June 2019, https://www.healthline.com/health-news/pregnant-women-arent-getting-the-vitamins-and-nutrients-they-need?msclkid=91a49710c15b11ec9fdf312770d44b13.

6. Dunsworth, H. M., Warrener, A. G., Deacon, T., Ellison, P. T., & Pontzer, H. (2012). Metabolic hypothesis for human altriciality. Proceedings of the National Academy of Sciences of the United States of America, 109(38), 15212–15216. https://doi.org/10.1073/pnas.1205282109

7. Sukumar N, Rafnsson SB, Kandala NB, Bhopal R, Yajnik CS, Saravanan P. Prevalence of vitamin B-12 insufficiency during pregnancy and its effect on offspring birth weight: a systematic review and meta-analysis. Am J Clin Nutr. 2016 May;103(5):1232-51. doi: 10.3945/ajcn.115.123083. Epub 2016 Apr 13. Erratum in: Am J Clin Nutr. 2017 Jan;105(1):241. PMID: 27076577.

Chapter 4

A higher prevalence of autistic people conceived in winter months

If a baby is conceived in the winter months they are 6% more likely to be autistic [1]. Autism B Theory explains that there is likely a correlation between a lack of vitamin D (the lack of sunlight in winter), and the biochemical pathways for vitamin B12.

Vitamin D is actually a hormone rather than a vitamin. It has been suggested that the current hormonal state of conception of the parents may be related to the hormonal state of the baby. Therefore, the lack of vitamin D may play a role in the future gut health and autoimmune development of the baby [2].

Vitamin D is mostly produced in the skin as a reaction to sunlight. Only 20% of vitamin D is absorbed through a healthy balanced diet, therefore natural sunlight is essential for gut health and B12 absorption.

A vitamin B 12 deficiency can result when the body is low in vitamin D. This is because there are vitamin D receptors in gut cells that make intrinsic factor needed for gut health. When vitamin D is low, intrinsic factor production becomes low and therefore the body is less able to absorb B12 from food [3]. This negatively impacts on healthy biochemical functions such as methionine cycles, SAM, methylation cycles, regulating glutamate levels, counteracting oxidative stress, reducing inflammation, and regulating methylmalonic acid (which helps protect cell membranes through things like adequate myelination of neurons).

The lack of sunlight (vitamin D) during winter months will therefore decrease the possibility of absorption of vitamin B12 within the gut. This could explain why there is a 6% increase of being autistic if conceived during winter months. This also highlights how low levels of vitamin B are likely to be involved in the natural cause of autism.

References

1. Zerbo, O., Iosif, A. M., Delwiche, L., Walker, C., & Hertz-Picciotto, I. [2011]. Month of conception and risk of autism. Epidemiology [Cambridge, Mass.], 22[4], 469–475. https://doi.org/10.1097/EDE.0b013e31821d0b53

2. Yang, C. Y., Leung, P. S., Adamopoulos, I. E., & Gershwin, M. E. [2013]. The implication of vitamin D and autoimmunity: a comprehensive review. Clinical reviews in allergy & immunology, 45[2], 217–226. https://doi.org/10.1007/s12016-013-8361-3

3. Gominak SC. Vitamin D deficiency changes the intestinal microbiome reducing B vitamin production in the gut. The resulting lack of pantothenic acid adversely affects the immune system, producing a "pro-inflammatory" state associated with atherosclerosis and autoimmunity. Med Hypotheses. 2016 Sep;94:103-7. doi: 10.1016/j.mehy.2016.07.007. Epub 2016 Jul 14. PMID: 27515213.

Chapter 5
The biochemical pathways involved with autism

This chapter highlights the probable biological origins of autism.

The long chains of chemical reactions that take place inside the body are described as biochemical pathways. The purpose of a pathway is to help the body maintain healthy functions. Although many pathways are reliant on many other pathways, some may be used immediately for certain body systems, as others may help make products needed for other pathways.

The Autism B Theory Biochemical Pathway Model (Figure 6) explains some of the pathways relating to vitamins B6, B9 and B12. Atypical development and functioning of these pathways can explain why some autistic people experience sensory sensitivities, a poor microbiome (gut health), epilepsy, chronic pain (fibromyalgia, neuralgic pain) and various other phenomena.

The human body cannot make vitamins B6, B9 and B12 on its own, it has to absorb them from dietary sources.

B6: fish, beef liver and other organ meats, potatoes, starchy vegetables and some fruits.

B9: dark green leafy vegetables (turnip greens, spinach, romaine lettuce, asparagus, Brussels sprouts, broccoli), beans, peanuts, sunflower seeds, some fresh fruits and whole grains.

B12: beef, liver, and chicken, fish and shellfish, eggs, and various dairy products.

Figure 6: Basic biochemical pathway.

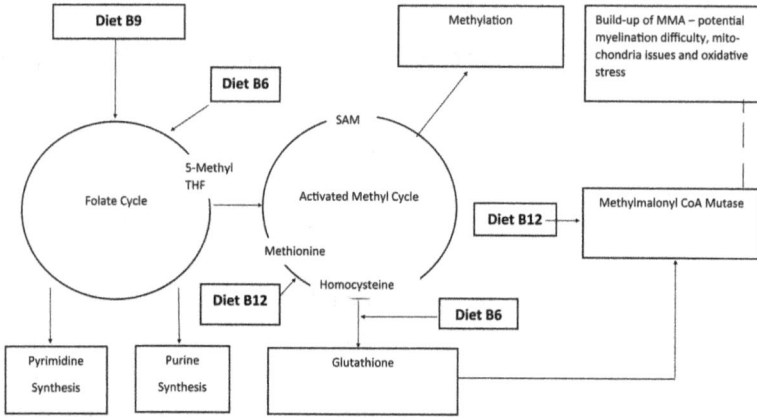

The Folate Cycle and the Activated Methyl Cycle are like circles, the continuously cycle to repeat their function to support overall health and wellbeing.

The Folate Cycle Pathway

Folate supports purine and pyrimidine synthesis as well as the Activated Methyl Cycle (discussed later). These biochemical pathways support red blood cells, cardiovascular health and nervous system functions.

The folate pathway is dependent on B9 (folate), and B6 (pyridoxine). One of the functions of the folate pathway is to support pyrimidine and purine synthesis. These systems are essential because they make the building blocks of DNA and RNA.

Purine and pyrimidine synthesis plays a major role in controlling embryonic and foetal development, specifically playing a role in controlling the myelination of neurons and cells. Abnormal functioning of purine and pyrimidine metabolism development can result in neurodivergence [1]. Interestingly, the purinergic control of neurodevelopment starts in the womb but is maintained after birth. If there has been a change to the expression and transmission of purine and pyrimidine metabolism during any time, then this can alter how genes express themselves (genetic alteration). For example, a period of time of low levels of B vitamins as a result of the biological demand of pregnancy, may be enough to alter gene expression for the developing baby. The alteration of genes is called epigenetics. Although not all genetic alterations are hereditarily passed to children, some are. The genetic alteration as a result of early atypical development could result in the baby passing this potential genetic variation to their future children should they have any. This can help start to explain the genetic link of autism.

If the folate pathway doesn't have enough B9 and B6 it will not function properly. This will likely result in a build-up of oxidative stress causing membrane damage to cells and neurons, epigenetic phenomena (meaning genes will develop atypically), as well as the potential for genetic mutation during early development. If this pathway does not cycle properly it could lead to the development of an autistic disposition.

The folate pathway also produces a substance called 5-Methyl tetrahydrofolate (THF) and passes this to the Activated Methyl Cycle. If the folate pathway doesn't cycle properly, then this will also prevent the Activated Methyl Cycle from functioning properly.

The Activated Methyl Cycle

The Activated Methyl pathway is crucial for early development and overall health. It is dependent on the folate pathway as well as vitamins B6 and B12.

The Activated Methyl pathway has many functions. The first thing is it helps create a substance called methionine. It basically does this by taking the 5-Methyl THF from the folate pathway, absorbing it with B12 to produce a substance called SAM which is needed for methylation functioning. Any SAM deficiency (as a result of low B6, B9 or B12), may result in atypical myelination and neuron connection.

Methylation is essential for early development and overall health. DNA methylation plays a key role by activating and silencing certain genes needed for the developing brain, the nervous system, genomic stability during mitosis (where a single cell divides into two identical daughter cells during early development), as well as the parent-of-origin imprinting. Again, low levels of B vitamins during early brain development will likely alter genetic signalling. This genetic alteration could result in the baby passing this genetic variant to their future children should they have any in adult life, which may help explain the genetic link involved with autism.

Poor methylation can result in various difficulties. For example, people may experience poor autoimmune health, allergies, poor microbiome (gut health), IBS, anxiety, depression, insomnia, headaches, poor bilirubin levels and musculature pain. In emergencies, additional choline and zinc nutrients are used to help support the Activated Methyl Cycle. However, if the Activated Methyl Cycle continues to run poorly, then all resources of zinc and choline may be used up which will result in a deficiency.

B12 plays a major role in the production of methionine which is required for methylation reactions. These reactions are essential for myelin maintenance and nerve function. The myelin helps protect and speed up communication between the different neurons within the brain and the wider nervous system.

Poor methylation, combined with low levels of B9 and B12, can result in neural tube defects such as intellectual disability and other neurodevelopmental conditions [2]. This may help explain the higher prevalence of autistic people in these populations.

After the Activated Methyl Cycle has supported methylation, it then goes on to help make and regulate levels of homocysteine. Vitamins B6, B9 and B12 are used to break down homocysteine to help create other chemicals the body needs, naturally reducing homocysteine levels. High homocysteine levels result in weakness, fatigue, tingling sensations (like pins and needles) and dizziness. It also increases the risk of dementia, heart disease and strokes. High homocysteine levels may mean a person has a vitamin deficiency in one or all three B vitamins (B6, B9 and B12). If there are safe levels of homocysteine, the extra B6 can then support the glutathione cycle.

Glutathione plays a key role in reducing oxidative stress, free radicals and antioxidants in the body. It also supports immune system functions, tissue building and helps make chemicals and proteins needed for the body. The glutathione pathway can't function well without support from folate and the Activated Methyl Cycle. Low levels of glutathione put a person at risk to toxins and toxic metals (a known cause of autism). Low levels will also compromise the autoimmune system, leaving the person vulnerable to gut issues, allergies, and other conditions prevalent within the autistic population such as a build-up of glutamate that can overexcite the brain.

The Activated Methyl Cycle, along with B12, also helps produce the chemicals needed to create Methylmalonyl-CoA mutase which helps regulate MMA levels (Methylmalonic acid). If there is not enough B12, then there will be a build-up of MMA. Small amounts of MMA are necessary for human metabolism and energy production, but too much is dangerous. A high amount of MMA typically means a vitamin B12 deficiency. Too much MMA will result in oxidative stress which will potentially damage the walls of cells and mitochondria which disrupts signalling between cells and neurons. Also, too much MMA will impact on the body's ability to produce myelin for neurons therefore resulting in atypically myelinated neurons. Atypically myelinated neurons may also impact on glial cells that help clear up excess glutamate. The mitochondria plays a significant role in meylination and also is dependent on key B vitamins. Anything that impacts this process will affect meylination development.

The Autism B Theory Biochemical Pathway Model (Figure 7), imposes the already known causes of autism, including Autism B Theory, on top of the biochemical pathways already discussed.

Figure 7: Basic biochemical pathway explaining Autism B theory and the known causes of autism.

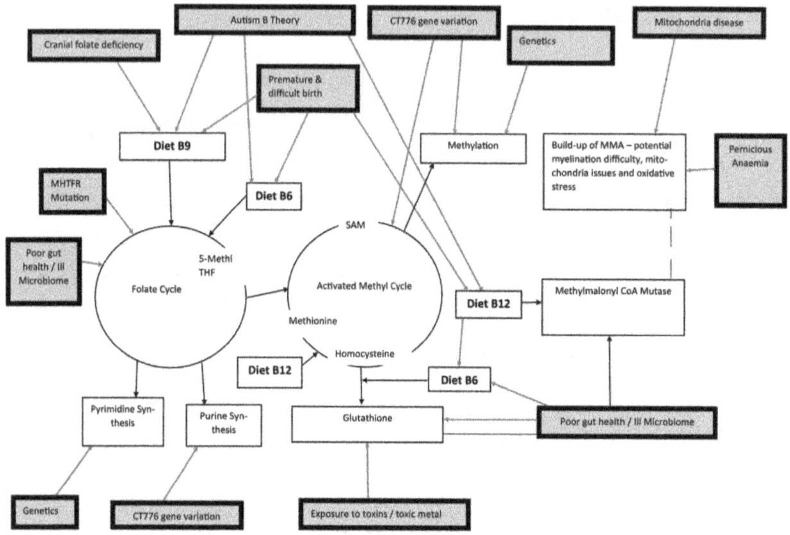

Epigenetic developments

Epigenetic developments take place during stages of development within the first few years of life. Such experiences result in epigenesis (creation of new gene alterations) which result in the production of new proteins which influence neural and biochemical pathways. As the development of autistic children is atypical, this means there will likely be atypical epigenesis in relation to neural and biochemical pathways. No two autistic people will be the same. This can explain why it is highly unlikely there will ever be a single gene responsible for autism.

Changes in any of the biochemical pathways may result in further genetic alterations. For example, play supports the growth of insulin-like growth factor-1 (IGF-1). Play may be of critical importance in the development of epigenesis. Play socialises the brain and this allows the creation of new gene expression to understand the emotional intent and actions of others, all which help create social intelligence. It also supports the development of executive functioning skills [3]. While also supporting musculoskeletal tissue, IGF-1 also plays a significant role in the nervous system growth and development. Theoretically, IGF-1 can have a positive impact on synaptic functioning (neurons communicating with each other, reduces neuronal excitability and may also improve oligodendrocytes myelination function). If autistic children engage in atypical play, then this will create atypical gene expression in relation to IGF-1 [4].

Autism B Theory hypothesises that low levels of B vitamins will impact biochemical pathways which will result in atypical development. Such difficulties highlighted in this chapter may result in associated health difficulties. Also, low levels of B vitamins may result in atypical myelination of some of the first developing neurons which can start to explain the diversity within the autism spectrum. A more in-depth analysis of the biochemical pathway for Autism B theory is in Appendix 3.

References

1. Fumagalli, Marta, et al. "Pathophysiological Role of Purines and Pyrimidines in Neurodevelopment: Unveiling New Pharmacological Approaches to Congenital Brain Diseases." Frontiers in Pharmacology, vol. 8, 2017, https://doi.org/10.3389/fphar.2017.00941.
2. Fumagalli, Marta, et al. "Pathophysiological Role of Purines and Pyrimidines in Neurodevelopment: Unveiling New Pharmacological Approaches to Congenital Brain Diseases." Frontiers in Pharmacology, vol. 8, 2017, https://doi.org/10.3389/fphar.2017.00941.
3. Panksepp, Jaak, et al. "Chapter 10." The Archaeology of Mind: Neuroevolutionary Origins of Human Emotions, W. W Norton, New York, 2012.
4. Bou Khalil, Rami. "The Potential Role of Insulin-like Growth Factor-1 and Zinc in Brain Growth of Autism Spectrum Disorder Children." Autism, vol. 23, no. 1, 2018, pp. 267–268., https://doi.org/10.1177/1362361317753565.

Chapter 6
Myelination of neurons

The human brain and wider nervous system have billions of neurons. These neurons transmit electrical signals down their axons to communicate with neighbouring neurons helping the brain communicate with the wider nervous system.

The main function of the nervous system is to take in, process and integrate the sensory information from the body and external environment. It does this so the brain can then instruct the various motor neurons to help the person move and act in the environment [1]. The nervous system is made up of two sub-systems (the central and peripheral), both consisting of myelinated neurons.

The central nervous system (CNS)

The CNS is located in the brain and spinal cord. It integrates information from the entire body, supporting sensory awareness and movement by continually updating the brain about what is happening inside and outside the body. The neurons of the CNS are myelinated oligodendrocytes. The oligodendrocyte neuron forms much more myelin (up to thirty times more) compared to Schwan cell neurons that are located in the peripheral nervous system.

The peripheral nervous system (PNS)

The myelinated neurons of the PNS are Schwann cells. They support the vast network of spine and cranial nerves, helping communicate sensory and motor information between the brain and body. This helps the brain perceive changes in the internal and external environment.

The PNS is divided into the autonomic and the somatic nervous systems. The autonomic nervous system has control of internal organs, blood vessels and smooth cardiac muscles. The somatic nervous system has voluntary control of skin, bones, joints, and skeletal muscle. The two systems function together by sending sensory and motor information from the PNS to the CNS through neurons.

Figure 3: A neuron.

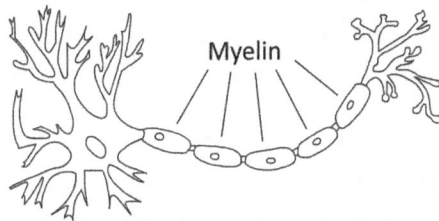

Communication between neurons is made through electrical signals. Electrical signals are sent down the axis (Nodes of Ranvier) of neurons that communicate with other neurons. The communication signal is received by the next neuron's dendrites, and this process is repeated with potentially millions of other neurons. These neuron connections wire the brain and nervous system together, particularly through sensitive and critical periods of development.

The longer the distance between the brain parts and wider nervous system, the greater the number of neuron connections needed. For example, a simple knee jerk involves millions of neurons. The knock triggers an electrical impulse that travels up sensory neurons to the spine. The spine then starts communicating with motor neurons, sending electrical signals back down to flex the leg. Communicating, socially interacting and problem-solving all require billions of sensory motor neurons that are much more complex compared with a simple knee-jerk reflex. Obviously these neurons need to communicate quickly to help the brain process information in real time. The thing that helps speed up communication is myelin.

Myelin is the white fatty sheath that forms around the axons of neurons and nerves in the brain and wider nervous system. Nerves are made of neurons [2]. Myelination protects and prevents electrical signals from leaking and connecting to other neurons (see Figure 8), enabling communication to be transported to the precise location in the quickest time possible. The communication speed of a neuron is between 120 to 240 kilometres per hour, with the average speed being around 180 kilometres. However, the speed of communication between neurons can be boosted by myelination. Myelinated neurons can communicate as fast as 432 kilometres per hour.

Myelination helps the brain integrate all sensory information with motor action. Unsurprisingly, atypically myelinated neurons will impact the brain's ability to fully integrate sensory information. For example, as people reach older age the myelin sheath covering the axons wears down which results in slower cognitive ability. Atypically myelinated neurons (the neurons seen at bottom of Figure 8) will be much slower passing electrical signals. Also, in some cases the communication signals may over connect with unintended neurons resulting in overconnectivity (resulting in fast processing to unintended neurons).

Figure 8: Different myelination of neurons.

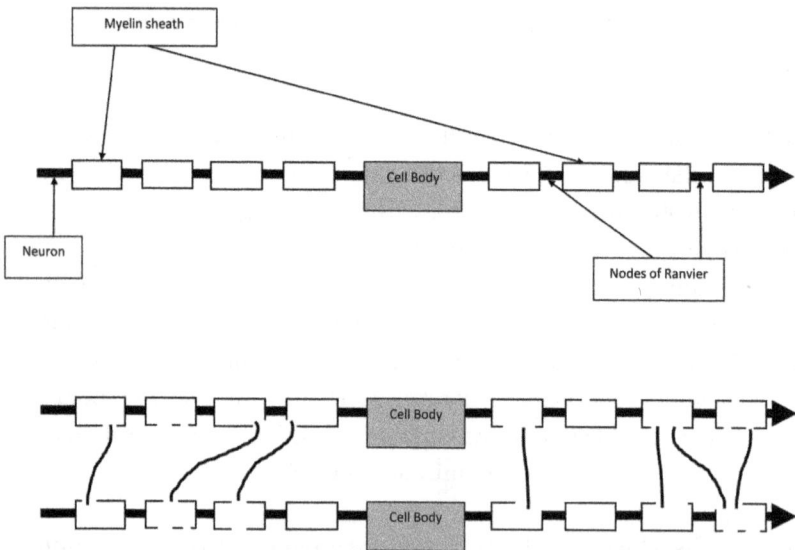

Myelin doesn't just pass on information, it supports the precise control and timing of sensory and motor communication between the brain and wider nervous system. Such timing and precision are essential, not only for motor skills and sensory awareness, but also for cognition and executive functioning skills. Even a delay of information processing by milliseconds can result in confusion and disorganisation [3]. The timing of neuron communication must be absolutely synchronised. Any delay in timing could result in poor sensory integration and possible cognitive dissonance.

Autism B Theory highlights the first developing neurons (sensory motor, mirror and social engagement neurons), may be atypically myelinated due to lower levels of vitamin B6, B9 or B12. The period of atypical myelination may have only happened for a particular period of time; and these periods of time will be different for each person. This can explain why there is such variation of myelination patterns seen across the autistic spectrum. As the baby grows and develops, subsequent connections of typical myelinated neurons are made on top of the unmyelinated ones, however, early atypical myelination can still affect neural communication and timing. There is various research that makes a correlation of atypical myelination patterns with levels of need and ability across the spectrum, for example, more atypical myelination may have a more profound effect on the brain. However, more research is needed to formally make this distinction.

References

1. Learning, Lumen. "Biology for Majors II." Lumen, https://courses.lumenlearning.com/wm-biology2/chapter/the-central-and-peripheral-nervous-systems/.
2. Lakna. "Difference between Nerve and Neuron: Definition, Types, Functions." Pediaa.Com, 13 July 2017, https://pediaa.com/difference-between-nerve-and-neuron/.
3. Kimura, Fumitaka, and Chiaki Itami. "Myelination and Isochronicity in Neural Networks." Frontiers, Frontiers, 1 Jan. 1AD, https://www.frontiersin.org/articles/10.3389/neuro.05.012.2009/full.

Chapter 7

Sensitive and critical periods of development: extra white matter and head size

The size of some autistic children's brains can be 5-10% larger compared with neurotypical children, as well as having a larger head circumference [1]. The difference in size starts to reduce after the first few years, eventually disappearing by adolescence. As well as a larger brain, there can be excess white matter in the brain for some autistic children [2].

Autism B Theory highlights two potential reasons why there may be an increased brain size and extra white matter. These are:

1. Reluctance to prune neurons during sensitive and critical periods of development.
2. Overconnectivity.

Reluctance to prune neurons during sensitive and critical periods of development

The larger brain and head circumference seen in some autistic children could be a result of atypical myelination during sensitive and critical periods of development.

What is the difference between sensitive and critical periods?

A sensitive period of development is when the brain is strongly influenced by experiences.

A critical period of development is when the brain has only a certain period of time to learn a skill. During a critical period, if the necessary experience is not available it becomes much harder, even impossible to acquire the skill after the time frame finishes. An example of a critical period is the ability to acquire language. People who missed the critical period of language development would not acquire their first language fluently [3]. Another example, if one eye (but not both) is covered after birth, even if the covering is brief, the covered eye will lose visual acuity permanently [4].

Two major factors influence sensitive and critical periods, these are neural maturation (the myelination and networking of neurons in the brain), and sensory experiences. Both need to coincide for critical periods of development.

A baby is born with 100 billion neurons, this is much more when compared to an adult. The excess neurons of early development help the brain develop quickly. Once sensitive and critical periods of development have taken place the brain starts to prune away the unused and unconnected neurons. This therefore explains why babies have more neurons compared with adults. A baby will grow about 250,000 nerve cells and neurons per minute throughout pregnancy. Each neuron can connect up to 15,000 other neurons to form neuro networks. Neurons in these networks are often myelinated as this helps support learning, memory and problem-solving. Myelination helps the brain learn from the environment faster than any other stage in life.

Various structures of the brain reach their peak of neuron connection within critical periods of development. For example, the visual cortex reaches its peak between the fourth and eighth month, but areas of the prefrontal cortex do not reach their peak until the fifteenth month. This demonstrates there are various critical periods for development.

It is as if evolution has given certain brain parts sensitive and critical periods to learn specific skills unconsciously before other brain areas undertake the next period of development. Sensitive and critical periods of development seem to happen in a linear process. By the time the baby is between two and three years old the brain starts to prune the excess neurons it no longer needs. This is because too many neurons can result in cross wiring, overconnectivity, excitability and unnecessary metabolic stress for the brain [5].

The autistic brain develops atypically, therefore it will not meet the sensitive and critical periods in linear fashion. This means the autistic brain will be reluctant to prune away neurons. This is because the sensitive and critical periods have still to be connected in the brain. The reluctance to prune may explain why there is extra cranial head size seen in some autistic children. However, eventually the pruning does take place. By the age of ten, about 50% of unused neuron connections will eventually be removed, and by mid adolescence most pruning takes place and this is when the head size of autistic children reduce to the same level as neurotypical children.

Overconnectivity

Another reason why there may be larger brains, or extra white matter, in developing autistic brains is because some neurons are over connecting as a result of atypical myelination.

The Nodes of Ranvier help pass communication down the axon of a neuron. If there are gaps due to atypically myelinated neurons, communication signals may be sent to unintended neurons, therefore resulting in overconnectivity which could explain the extra brain size in early development.

Figure 8: Different myelination of neurons.

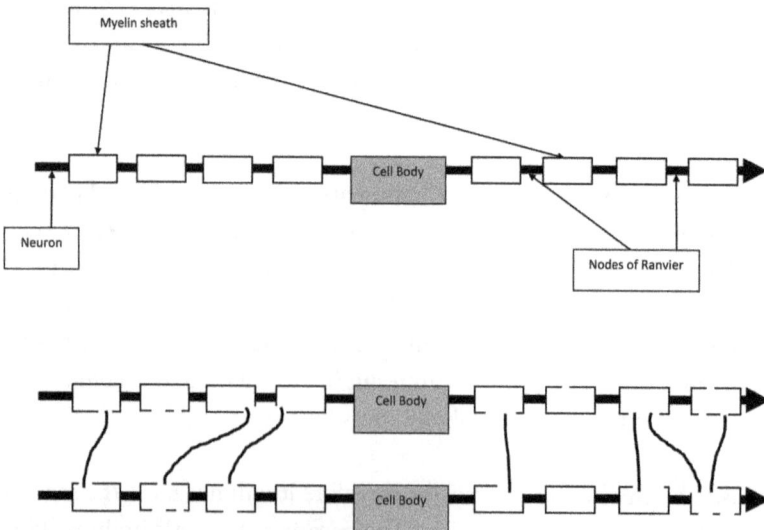

Overconnectivity as a result of atypically myelinated neurons may explain extra white matter in some developing autistic brains [6]. The atypical connection of neurons will make it difficult for the brain to know what neuronal networks to prune. This is why pruning takes much longer in autism, explaining why there is periods of extra white matter and larger head size for some autistic children [7]. The reluctance to prune neurons will mean there is additional time for critical periods of development to catch up. The additional time will mean some neurons will be over connecting to other neurons. Also, extra white matter connectivity may help explain synaesthesia. See Appendix 5 (Synaesthesia and Irlen Syndrome) for a fuller explanation.

If the overconnectivity is intense, it will result in too many connections being made. This could impact on the brains ability to coordinate neural networks and will therefore impact on cognitive and IQ ability as well as contribute to a higher prevalence rate of epilepsy [8, 9].

However, a degree of overconnectivity that does not overwhelm the brain of some autistic people may help their brain connect quicker which could lead to advanced cognitive and intellectual ability. This can start to explain why some autistic people may meet some milestones early, have impressive memory recall and islets of ability, yet these people may still be autistic due to atypically myelinated Social Engagement Neurons which means social interactions are difficult (discussed later).

Even autistic people with a perceived low IQ can have special islets of ability which would be beyond a person with a low IQ. This is why there should be no predetermined IQ assumption when supporting autistic people.

An easy way to help understand why there may be extra white matter in the autistic brain is by using the analogy of hardware and software in relation to the grey and white areas of the brain. The hardware is the grey matter within the brain, and the software is the white matter. In essence, the grey matter is where the processing is done, and the white matter is the communication highways between the grey.

Figure 9: White and grey matter in the brain.

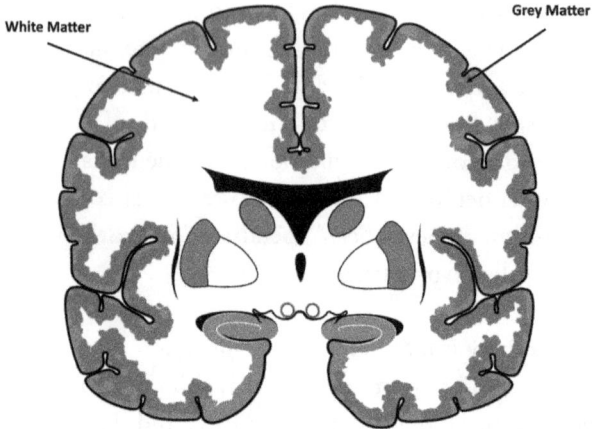

The grey matter (hardware) consists primarily of neuronal cell bodies, the structure that houses the neuron's nucleus which does the computation. These cell bodies are mostly non-myelinated, which is why they are grey.

The white matter consists of myelinated neurons. These neurons are called white matter because myelin is a white fatty substance. These neurons are like highways between the grey areas of the brain. The myelinated neurons pass communication between different parts of grey matter. If there are atypical myelination patterns of white matter then this will result in atypical cognitive functioning. For example, too much traffic is being processed in certain parts of the brain, while other areas may not be receiving enough traffic.

The level of atypical myelination will likely corelate to the diverse spectrum of autistic differences [10]. Diversity goes in all directions, including high and low IQ as seen within the autistic spectrum. The intensity of atypical myelination patterns may result in more demand on brain processing, higher prevalence of sensory sensitivity, social communication challenges and potentially intellectual disabilities.

For other autistic people, atypical myelination may also result in extra connectivity which may develop higher intellectual abilities. However, regardless of the intellectual ability the autistic person will likely struggle with sensory sensitivity and elements of social communication in neurotypical environments.

There is ongoing research that links increased epilepsy to different myelination patterns, overconnectivity and excess glutamate (discussed in chapter 5). A combination of all three help explain the increased epilepsy prevalence within the autistic population.

References

1. Roth, Ilona. "Page 166." The Autism Spectrum in the 21st Century: Exploring Psychology, Biology and Practice, Jessica Kingsley in Association with the Open University, London, 2010.
2. "Autism's Relationship to Head Size, Explained." Spectrum, 6 Aug. 2020, https://www.spectrumnews.org/news/ autisms-relationship-to-head-size-explained/.
3. "Extra-Thick Connections Mark Brains of Toddlers with Autism: Spectrum: Autism Research News." Spectrum, 21 Sept. 2015, https://www.spectrumnews.org/news/ extra-thick-connections-mark-brains-of-toddlers-with-autism/.
4. Robson AL (2002). "Critical/Sensitive Periods". In Salkind NJ (ed.). Child Developent. Gale Virtual Reference Library. New York: Macmillan Reference USA.
5. Hensch TK. Critical period plasticity in local cortical circuits. Nat Rev Neurosci. 2005 Nov;6(11):877-88. doi: 10.1038/nrn1787. PMID: 16261181.
6. Zikopoulos, B., & Barbas, H. (2010). Changes in prefrontal axons may disrupt the network in autism. The Journal of neuroscience : the official journal of the Society for Neuroscience, 30(44), 14595–14609. https://doi.org/10.1523/JNEUROSCI.2257-10.2010
7. Andrews, D. S., Avino, T. A., Gudbrandsen, M., Daly, E., Marquand, A., Murphy, C. M., Lai, M. C., Lombardo, M. V., Ruigrok, A. N., Williams, S. C., Bullmore, E. T., The Mrc Aims

Consortium, Suckling, J., Baron-Cohen, S., Craig, M. C., Murphy, D. G., & Ecker, C. (2017). In Vivo Evidence of Reduced Integrity of the Gray-White Matter Boundary in Autism Spectrum Disorder. Cerebral cortex (New York, N.Y. : 1991), 27(2), 877–887. https://doi.org/10.1093/cercor/bhw404

8. Godel Michel, Andrews Derek S., Amaral David G., Ozonoff Sally, Young Gregory S., Lee Joshua K., Wu Nordahl Christine, Schaer Marie. (2021). Altered Gray-White Matter Boundary Contrast in Toddlers at Risk for Autism Relates to Later Diagnosis of Autism Spectrum Disorder. Frontiers in Neuroscience, Volume 15. URL=https://www.frontiersin.org/article/10.3389/fnins.2021.669194 DOI=10.3389/fnins.2021.669194

9. Buckley AW, Holmes GL. Epilepsy and Autism. Cold Spring Harb Perspect Med. 2016 Apr 1;6[4]:a022749. doi: 10.1101/cshperspect.a022749. PMID: 26989064; PMCID: PMC4817741.

10. Hogan R. E. (2020). Epilepsy as a Disease of White Matter. Epilepsy currents, 21(1), 27–29. https://doi.org/10.1177/1535759720975744).

Chapter 8
Myelination of sensory motor neurons

There are various ages and stages for development. For simplicity, this book will be focusing on three main stages.

Figure 10: Stages of development.

Stages of development
Sensory motor: 0-2 years.
Social emotional: 2-3 years.
Social development with others: 3-5 years.

Motor neurons help kickstart sensory motor awareness [1, 2]; the foundation for all future sensitive and critical periods of development. For example, a baby is born with automated reflexes such as gripping and sucking and it is from these basic movements that helps the baby grow and learn. If these early neurons are atypically myelinated, then the baby will likely grow up with sensory sensitivities, including an under sensitivity with motor movement. Increasing research is demonstrating a lack of voluntary motor movement in autistic babies [3].

It is proposed there is a neuro map of the body which is created during the sensory motor stage of development [4]. The neuro map is developed through sensory motor exploration in the environment. This neuro map helps the brain understand what actions the body is capable of. This exploration helps the brain understand what the external physical world is like. This awareness is often referred to as embodied knowledge.

Another example of embodied knowledge is imitation. The act of imitation is not just copying what others are doing, instead, it is about developing a sense of embodied knowledge about how to act in the environment. Imitation happens before a baby is consciously aware of what they are doing. Eventually babies start to build memory systems of what they have been imitating as this helps them associate words with actions, people and objects. In time they can start to abstract from these words which helps develop their social and cognitive skills. This process of learning all starts with motor movement (myelinated motor neurons).

Figure 11: Cognitive development from
sensory motor movement upwards [2,3].

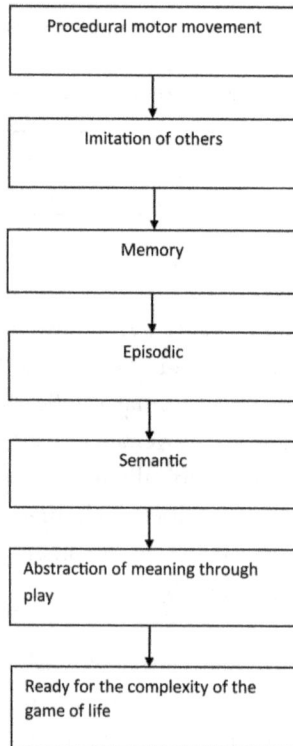

Procedural motor movement

↓

Imitation of others

↓

Memory

↓

Episodic

↓

Semantic

↓

Abstraction of meaning through play

↓

Ready for the complexity of the game of life

The neuro map of the body must be able to integrate the external sensory stimulation (noise, vision and touch) with the proprioception sense (the sense of body and position). If there are atypically myelinated motor neurons, then some of the external sensory information may not be fully integrated by the brain within the synchronised and precision timing as it should. For example, the person may be only able to focus on one sensory system at any one time, have difficulty changing focus and likely experience sensory overload.

Sensory sensitivities

Up to 70% of all information sent to the brain is done so through motor pathways [5]. This validates how important a body is in relation to perception, action and cognition. If motor neurons are atypically myelinated, then this could result in a fragmented (or delayed) perception of sensory experiences. Naturally, the brain will want to have a better perception of what the fragmented sensory experiences are, and will therefore add additional stress receptors around certain senses to make them much more sensitive. The additional stress receptors help the brain register the sensory experiences much faster. However, by doing so, the added stress receptors develop hypersensitivities for certain sensory experiences.

Alternatively, if the brain is experiencing a sense to intensely, again it may add additional stress receptors. This time it does so to alert the person to intense sensations as quickly as possible. This is because the sensory experience overwhelms the brain, therefore the brain wants alerted to the intense sensation quickly as it may help the person avoid overexposure more quickly in the future. Again, this will result in further sensory sensitivities for the person.

Hypersensitive

If the eyes (or head) do not move enough during early development then there is a chance of developing a sensitivity to certain lights. This is because people can become temporarily blind if they continue to look at something without moving their eyes (the light starts to burn the retina). If the baby doesn't voluntarily move their head or eyes enough during early development, then the brain may add more stress receptors in relation to light, therefore creating sensitivity.

If the ears and head don't move enough to help locate or distinguish certain sounds, then the brain may add stress receptors creating a sensitivity to certain noises.

Smaller ear muscles are needed to understand tonality, pitch and emotion within verbal communication. If the sensory motor neurons within the inner ear are atypically myelinated during sensitive and critical periods, then the person may have future difficulty hearing or expressing emotions in voices. This may even result in the person developing a monotone vocal sound.

If the motor neurons don't send information quickly to the brain about what is in the mouth, then it is likely the mouth is going to become highly sensitised. The brain will add more stress receptors in relation to taste and texture to help understand what is in the mouth better. This will create sensitivity which could result in a restricted diet.

If the head and nose muscles don't move enough to help locate or distinguish certain smells, then the nose may become more sensitised.

The brain usually needs motor movement to understand the sensation of objects that come into contact with the skin (soft, hard, smooth, rough, hot or cold). As a result of an under sensitive motor system, more stress receptors will be located on the skin to help the brain understand what is touching the skin. This can explain why some people become sensitive to certain clothes, textures, labels, socks, showers, temperature, detergent and bedding.

The only sense it seems a person cannot be over-sensitised with is the proprioceptive sense. Instead, it seems almost all autistic people are under sensitive in this sense (proprioceptive receptors are located in all the muscles and tendons which help the brain know how to move the body). This is why there is more and more research highlighting the lack of voluntary muscle control in babies as a potential sign for developing autism [1].

Hyposensitivity

The brain may not receive enough sensory information because of the delay in information being sent through motor pathways as a result of atypically myelinated neurons. Instead of adding stress receptors, some autistic brains will instruct the person to seek extra experiences to help understand the sense better. This will mean the person will then seek out extra sensory stimulation for those experiences. For example, some people may seek out certain lights, smells, tastes, textures and body movement, some may avoid them.

This can start to explain why there is so much variation in sensory sensitivities within the autistic spectrum. Some people may be oversensitive with some senses but under-responsive (sensory seeking) with others.

Atypically myelinated motor neurons can explain why autistic people often have a difficulty with interoception senses (sensations within the body such as thirst, hunger, pain, time, feelings and toilet needs). The delay in information sent to the brain through motor pathways may result in the autistic brain not realising they have pain, are hungry, thirsty or feel the need to go to the toilet. Eventually the autistic brain senses a threshold and will flood the person with feelings to act in relation to these interoception needs.

The autistic brain needs extra proprioceptive input to help function

The brain needs to know where body parts are at all times as this helps the brain to decide what to do, how to act and keep safe. The brain knows where the body parts are because of proprioceptive receptors located in the muscles and tendons. The proprioception system works unconsciously. If the brain does not get enough body feedback, it will likely instruct the body to move to activate the proprioceptive receptors. This then gives the brain a reference point of where the body parts are should they be needed for action. For example, when someone experiences a dead leg, the brain will force the person to keep prodding the leg as the increased proprioceptive feedback helps inform the brain where the body parts are.

It seems as if the brain has 0.2 seconds to unconsciously process what to do when faced with a demand (this could be a result of something new, a change of plan or something new to physically interact with in the environment), described by Benjamin Libet as the neural time factor [6, 7]. In relation to a demand, the brain will access the motor cortex to identify what motor actions are needed to deal with the demand. If the brain can successfully identify what motor movements it needs within 0.2 seconds, the person will act out the motor movement with little conscious awareness. This is because when the brain has good proprioceptive feedback from the body it can decide what to do quickly. This highlights that even for a person to mentally think of how to act (executive function skills), even unconsciously, the brain needs full use of proprioceptive senses.

If the brain doesn't have good proprioceptive feedback, as is the case for autistic people, then it will have difficulty trying to decide what to do when faced with a new demand (something new, a change). If the brain takes longer than 0.2 seconds to decide what motor movement is needed to overcome the new situation or change, it will automatically start to prepare all the emotional systems. This is because emotional arousal helps the person focus on what may help overcome the demand. As each 0.2 second passes, the more heightened the emotional systems become. This is the start of the fight, flight or freeze responses.

Figure 12: Panksepp seven emotional systems [8, 9].

Emotional system (Panksepp Affective Neuroscience)						
Seeking	Play	Fear	Grief/Panic	Rage	Lust	Care
Motivated, arousal, interested to seek change, curious	Joy, glee, happy, socially engaging, laughter, sense of humour	Anxiety, phobias, panic, trauma, worry	Separation distress, sadness, guilt, shame, embarrassment, poor-self image	Anger, irritability, rage	Erotic feelings, attraction	Nurturance, care, love

The reason why this starts to happen within 0.2 seconds is because hesitation, from an evolutionary perspective, could result in a fatal injury. Ancient ancestors needed to make decisions quickly in situations to stay alive. For example, the shaking bush may have been a predator, so better being quick (0.2 seconds) with decision making to stay alive. Humans today still have that old brain circuitry of 0.2 seconds to make decisions before experiencing emotions, even for the arbitrary basic demands of modern life.

As each 0.2 seconds pass, the old brain areas responsible for survival will try and encourage the executive functioning area of the brain to stop engaging with the new situation (or demand) and revert back to something more predictable and safe. It does this by generating negative emotions (fear, grief and panic systems highlighted in Figure 12), as this will likely stop the person going ahead with a decision that may be harmful. It is as if the brain is saying, "*better to miss out on anything new because the new thing could be fatal, so stick with what you know*".

The executive functioning area works with the motor area of the brain to determine if the body has the musculature ability to act out the instructions. If possible, the motor area of the brain will inform the executive function area that it can act out its hypothetical mental instruction that it generated. The motor area then integrates all the sensory information needed for the muscles (proprioception and precise myelinated sensory motor neuron patterns) to act out the mental instruction. What is then observed is behaviour [10].

As autistic people often have proprioceptive needs (an under-regulated sensory motor system), then obviously it will take the autistic brain longer than 0.2 seconds (to engage the atypically myelinated patterns of motor neurons) to determine the most appropriate decision of what to do within a new situation or change. The difficulty that autistic people experience is that their brain will start to activate all the emotional systems more and more as each 0.2 seconds pass. This can often mean panic, anger and fear is experienced when faced with a new situation or change.

It is when things are unplanned, or changed suddenly, that creates anxiety for autistic people. This is because the autistic brain has difficulty integrating all the sensory information needed (arranging atypically myelinated neurons) to change focus, emphasise attention, problem solve and make a decision. Even small changes can throw an autistic person. For example, a change of seat, new equipment, a different cup, a new toothbrush, a new bed, a new computer or change of room could all result in extreme stress due to the different sensory motor neurons the brain needs to arrange before panic and anxiety starts (0.2 seconds).

If autistic people are sensitively supported with extra time to process, clear instructions, sound logic and potential use of visual instruction, then it helps the autistic brain anticipate what the changes are. This helps activate the motor neurons needed to fully utilise executive functioning skills. This is why timetables, social stories, now & next cards, visual timetables, verb words, modelling, cartoon scripting, videos and various other visual methods can be helpful for autistic people as they all help the brain engage the motor areas needed to support executive function skills before anxiety systems are activated.

Stimming behaviour can also support executive functioning skills. The stimming behaviour (rocking, bouncing, pressure on muscles and joints, spinning, swings and tapping) all help the brain have a better reference point of proprioceptive receptors. This helps the brain engage the sensory motor neurons within 0.2 seconds which means the autistic person can think clearer and use executive functioning skills without apprehension, anxiety or panic.

References

1. Peterson, Jordan B. "Chapter 2." Maps of Meaning, Taylor and Francis, S.I., 2002.
2. Empathy, Play and the Social Regulation of Aggression – Jordan Peterson. https://www.jordanbpeterson.com/docs/230/2014/19Petersonplay.pdf. https://www.scholastic.com/parents/family-life/social-emotional-learning/development-milestones/social-development-3-5-year-olds.html
3. Torres, E. and Whyatt, C., 2018. Autism: The movement-sensing perspective. 1st ed. Boca Raton : CRC Press, Taylor & Francis Group, (2018).
4. Panksepp, Jaak, et al. "Chapter 2." The Archaeology of Mind: Neuroevolutionary Origins of Human Emotions, W. W Norton, New York, 2012, p. 69.

5. David, Alfred. The Secret Life of the Brain: Unlocking the Mysteries of the Mind, Cassell, London, 2019, p. 99.

6. Libet B. How does conscious experience arise? The neural time factor. Brain Res Bull. 1999 Nov-Dec;50(5-6):339-40. doi: 10.1016/s0361-9230(99)00143-4. PMID: 10643426.

7. McGilchrist, Iain. "Chapter 5, The Primacy of the Right Hemisphere ." Master and His Emissary: The Divided Brain and the Making of the Western World, Yale University Press, 2019.

8. Panksepp, Jaak. "The Neuro-Evolutionary Cusp between Emotions and Cognitions." Consciousness and Emotion, vol. 1, no. 1, 2000, pp. 15–54., https://doi.org/10.1075/ce.1.1.04pan.

9. Panksepp, Jaak. Affective Neuroscience: The Foundations of Human and Animal Emotions. Oxford University Press, 2014.

10. Panksepp, Jaak. "Chapter 11." Affective Neuroscience: The Foundations of Human and Animal Emotions, Oxford University Press, Oxford Et Al., 2014, p. 413.

Chapter 9

Social engagement neurons and cranial nerves

Autistic people often have difficulty learning social skills such as understanding emotional intentions, reading facial expressions, understanding body language and social flexibility. Some autistic people may have alexithymia, and some may have difficulties with facial recognition (prosopagnosia).

How do people express emotion such as facial expressions of happiness, sadness or anger? How do people understand their own emotional regulation and that of others? The answer to these questions can be discovered by exploring the Social Engagement System.

The Social Engagement System

The term Social Engagement System was developed by Stephen Porges in relation to his work around polyvagal theory [1]. The Social Engagement System is a complex set of neural nerves that connect the brain to the face, eyes, throat, ears, lungs, heart and gut. Some of the very first neurons that are myelinated are within these nerves. The successful connection of all these nerves and neurons helps the brain express emotion, as well as having the ability to understand the emotional intention of self and others. This obviously helps develop social communication skills.

The Social Engagement System is made from the twelve cranial nerves (discussed later). Each cranial nerve has many functions, but some are key for developing social skills.

Neurons and nerves, what are the difference?

A neuron is a cell of the nervous system that conducts nerve impulses to help facilitate communication. Nerves are made of neurons. Nerves help the brain coordinate muscle movement, as well as helping the brain develop overall feelings of sensations in and around the body. Both neurons and nerves are foundational parts of the nervous system [2].

Twelve cranial nerves

The brain has twelve cranial nerves. These nerves work together and are a mixture of both sensory and motor neurons. The sensory and motor information from these neurons is sent to the brain where they are integrated for overall perception.

Sensory cranial nerves help a person to see, smell and hear.

Motor cranial nerves help control muscle movements of the face, head and neck which help express and understand facial expressions, emotions, tonality and pitch in communication.

All the cranial neurons and nerves are myelinated apart from the optic (for sight) and olfactory (for smell) nerves. The cranial nerves that are myelinated are done so during the first months of life and therefore could be atypically myelinated as discussed in previous chapters.

It is best to initially look at the 7th and 10th cranial nerves to help understand how humans socially interact with each other. Further exploration of the other ten cranial nerves is discussed later.

The 7th cranial nerve: The facial nerve

The 7th cranial nerve is one of the most important for the expression and understanding of emotion. There are roughly 10,000 neurons within the 7th cranial nerve, and around 7,000 of these are myelinated.

Here is a breakdown of some of the 7th cranial nerve (neurons) muscles and functions:

- Frontalis: forehead movement.
- Corrugator: brow movement.
- Nasalis: nose movement.
- Orbicularis oculi: eye wrinkle movement.
- Levator labii, Orbicularis oris, Risorius, Buccinator, Depressor labii and Levator anguli oris: lip movement.
- Mentalis: chin movement.

All are needed to help express emotion on the face, as well as understand the emotional expression of other people (you can only emotionally empathise when you have experienced similar emotions). Atypical myelination of these individual neurons may result in difficulty for the person expressing emotion. For example, someone may have difficulty expressing emotions with eyes, facial expressions, prosody of speech (monotone), and/or have difficulty integrating all these social signals at any one time.

Difficulties understanding facial emotions and prosody can help explain why some autistic people have a tendency for things such as anime, Pokémon, Thomas the Tank Engine, Ruff-Ruff Tweet, Mario, Transformers and various other slapstick cartoon or comedy characters. These characters have very obvious prosody and delayed facial expressions which helps emphasise the intended emotion and intention of the character which makes it easier to understand them. Also, these characters are often one dimensional which makes their behaviour predictable. Obviously there is various psychological and philosophical meanings within character behaviour, but it is likely the delayed and obvious facial expressions is what initially interests some autistic people.

Pitch, tone and prosody of speech

As mammals evolved from reptiles, their middle ear bones detached from their jawbone, helping the ear to have a better range for hearing emotion. When the muscles around the eyes display emotion (the orbicularis oculi wrinkles), it also tenses the middle ear muscles allowing the person to hear the emotional intentions of others better during social interactions. The same process happens when someone is singing. It is very hard to express emotion through voice without moving facial muscles [3].

Atypically myelinated neurons within the 7th cranial nerve will impact on the person's ability to express, and understand, emotion through facial expression and speech. Also, atypical myelination of the 7th cranial nerve for facial expressions can also explain why humour, sarcasm and non-literal use of words can often be difficult for some autistic people.

Eye contact

Some autistic people have difficulty recognising the positive aspects of social emotion in the face. This can help explain why some autistic people feel eye contact is overwhelming. The brain (including the autistic brain) seems to have the hard wired ability to detect sclera (the white part of the eye) [3]. The ability to detect sclera helps determine fear or surprise in others. This is helpful because fear and surprise is often associated with potential threat or danger. However, as some autistic people may struggle to detect the wider facial expressions (due to atypically myelinated 7th cranial nerves), it is possible their brain will only detect the white part of the eyes and not the wider context (facial expressions of tone, pitch and body language). This may mean some autistic brains will only perceive fear or surprise (the brain is only registering white sclera and not the wider context of communication) when social interacting with others, often resulting in feelings of fear and anxiety.

The 10th cranial nerve: The vagal nerve

The 10th cranial nerve is called the vagal nerve. A significant number of neurons within the vagal nerve are myelinated. The vagal nerve is the longest of all the twelve cranial nerves. It is sometimes referred to as the vagus or wandering nerve. This is because it travels from the brain and connects to the face, ears, throat, heart, lungs and gut. Why would the vagal nerve be connected to so many things?

Historically, the vagal nerve was only connected to the fight, flight and freeze responses. Through evolution some mammals evolved from reptiles into humans. Although humans are very different to reptiles, they still share the same ancient circuitry of the fight, flight and freeze responses. The vagal nerve helps detect potential danger through perception of angry faces, negative tone and closed body language.

Figure 13: Reptile fight, flight freeze response.

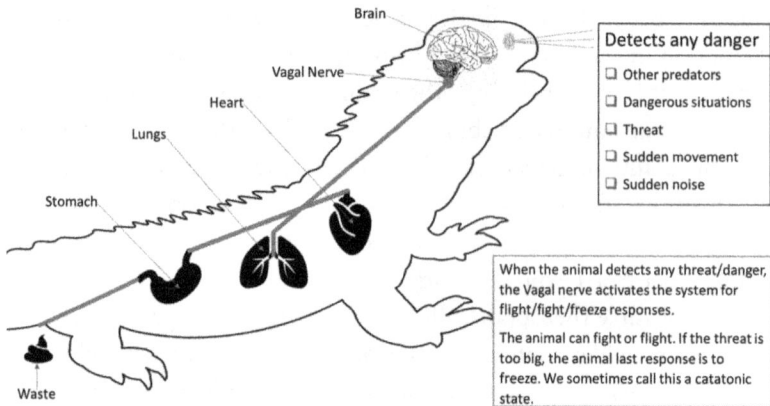

Brain

Vagal Nerve

Heart

Lungs

Stomach

Waste

Detects any danger
- Other predators
- Dangerous situations
- Threat
- Sudden movement
- Sudden noise

When the animal detects any threat/danger, the Vagal nerve activates the system for flight/fight/freeze responses.

The animal can fight or flight. If the threat is too big, the animal last response is to freeze. We sometimes call this a catatonic state.

As mammals evolved to become more social, there had to be more than the fight, flight or freeze response of the vagal nerve. Connections from the vagal nerve helped coordinate all the cranial nerves to work together, enabling humans to communicate socially and emotionally with each other.

This system is now described as the Social Engagement System [1]. This helped people understand the emotional state of others which informed them who was trustworthy and who was dangerous.

Figure 14: Human Social Engagement System.

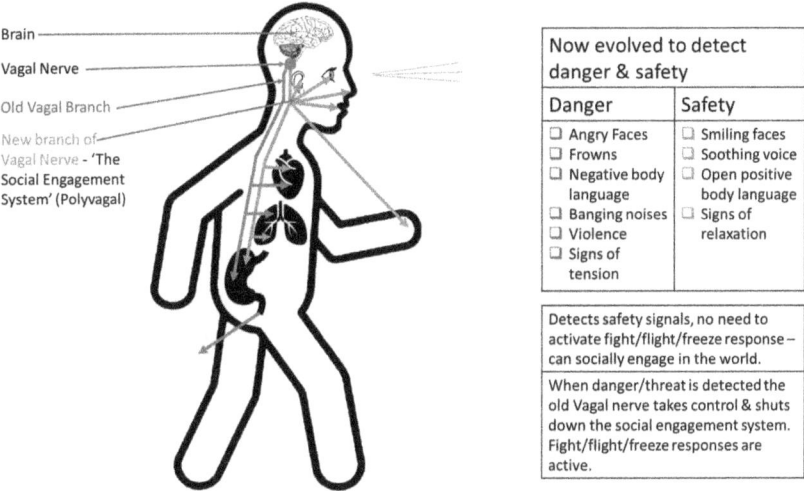

Brain	
Vagal Nerve	
Old Vagal Branch	
New branch of Vagal Nerve - 'The Social Engagement System' (Polyvagal)	

Now evolved to detect danger & safety	
Danger	Safety
☐ Angry Faces ☐ Frowns ☐ Negative body language ☐ Banging noises ☐ Violence ☐ Signs of tension	☐ Smiling faces ☐ Soothing voice ☐ Open positive body language ☐ Signs of relaxation

Detects safety signals, no need to activate fight/flight/freeze response – can socially engage in the world.
When danger/threat is detected the old Vagal nerve takes control & shuts down the social engagement system. Fight/flight/freeze responses are active.

It seems as if the vagal nerve has evolved to have two states. One is of safety, and the other is the activation of the fight, flight or freeze response. Only one state can be activated at any one time [1].

If someone is being friendly they will usually be smiling, projecting open body language, using a friendly tone and generally calm. The Social Engagement System detects these positive signals and perceives them as signs of safety, it as if it is telling the brain, "*there is no danger present, you can relax*". The brain then releases oxytocin, serotonin and dopamine. Oxytocin is often referred to as the love hormone, but this is misleading. Instead, oxytocin is what makes people feel more confident around other people [3]. Serotonin supports satiated feelings of calmness, and dopamine gives confidence and motivation to move and explore. All three are needed for positive social interactions.

As humans share this Social Engagement System with other mammals (for example dogs and horses), it becomes evident why things such as pet therapy can have a calming influence on people.

Alternatively, if someone is being hostile they will have an angry tone, frowning and will project negative body language. The Social Engagement System detects these signals as danger in the environment and will start to shut down the production of oxytocin, serotonin and dopamine. The brain will start releasing adrenalin (also known as epinephrine) which starts to activate the fight, flight and freeze responses. It is as if the Social Engagement System is saying, *"potential danger present, let's get the body prepared for conflict"*.

Fight, flight and freeze responses

The fight response prepares the body for action to fight off danger.

The flight response prepares the body to take off should the danger be too big.

The freeze response is used if the person cannot fight or run away. During this response the gut loosens and the bowels empty. This hopefully deceives the predator to think *"Don't eat or go close as it's possibly decomposing"*. Eventually, the body comes out of the faint or freeze response to live another day.

Humans still have this ancient system of safety which can be activated when experiencing less severe dangers such as speaking in public or socially interacting. The freeze response is sometimes referred to as catatonia or a catatonic state. This state is likely the basis for situational mutism in relation to autistic people who find social situations and change overwhelming. For example, talking in class, speaking at a meeting or dealing with authority figures often make people self-conscious, even to the point they start to experience situational mutism or catatonia.

To help fuel the fight, flight or freeze responses, the brain will start to shut down the processes of the gut as this frees up more energy to deal with the potential threat. The brain will inform the gut to defecate what is there. This helps explain why people experience embarrassing personal care situations when under extreme stress. It is as if the brain is saying *"It is better to have all energy to deal with danger, and if that means poor gut health for the next few moments, then so be it"*.

Even short sharp inhales of breath can activate the fight, flight or freeze responses. This is because any attempt at getting oxygen into the body quickly is a signal to the brain that action of the muscles may be imminent. Alternatively, slow exhales start to reduce the fight, flight and freeze responses. It is as if the brain thinks the person must not perceive danger because they are voluntary reducing the need for large amounts of oxygen and therefore the nervous system can relax. This is why breathing work within disciplines such as meditation, yoga, humming and chanting are all good practices to settle an overactive nervous system.

The brain is primed for negative emotion before positive. For example, it is better to look to avoid threats to help stay alive before engaging in new opportunities. As some autistic people may have difficulty understanding the wider context of positive social communication (smiling faces, relaxed tone and positive body language), but only detect the white sclera of eyes, then the autistic brain will at times unconsciously perceive danger in social situations even when there is none. This is because the main thing the autistic brain is perceiving is the sclera, and without the context of the wider face or body language, sclera signals surprise and threat. Such perception of surprise or threat can start to activate the fight, flight or freeze responses when around other people.

Any sensitive autism support should focus on opening the positive system of the Social Engagement System. This would include a soft-spoken tone, smiling face and positive body language. Any negative display (such as frowns, loud voices, angry tone and negative body language) will likely cause unnecessary anxiety.

More autistic males than females and autistic masking

There seems to be more autistic males diagnosed compared to females. The exact reasons are unknown, but atypical myelination can provide an insight. Males seem to have more myelinated neurons in early development compared to females [4].

Although males have more myelinated neurons in early development, females have more turnover of myelinated neurons in later development. The reason for this difference is unknown but it is likely oestrogen plays a role.

Oestrogen is a hormone that plays an important role in the normal sexual and reproductive development in women. Oestrogen seems to help with generating new myelin. It seems males only have their Social Engagement System myelinated once (during early infancy). However, females have two opportunities for myelinating their Social Engagement System, one in early infancy and another at the pre-teen stage of development [5]. For example, during puberty (8-15 years) the female body produces more oestrogen, which may help remyelinate neurons within the Social Engagement System [6]. The second myelination period could help develop social skills, partly explaining why females are more social than males. As females may be more social can start to explain why there is a higher prevalence of masking within the autistic female population. Masking is when someone is trying to mask their autistic traits in order to fit in socially. It often comes at a cost, resulting in experiences of stress, burnout and confusion. This means females are often acutely aware they are different when in neurotypical company, especially when they have not discovered they are autistic. Environments such as school, college, work or social settings will often be difficult. Females will know that they are different and this may start inner feelings of conflict which therefore makes them vulnerable to poor mental health, hence why they may start the process of masking. The same thing can happen for males, it is just more prevalent for females.

It has been well researched that children who do not meet critical social development milestones between three to five years will likely have social interaction difficulties for the rest of their life [7,8]. According to Erikson, if these critical periods of social development are not met, the child will become fearful, socially excluded, limited in their ability to play and become negatively dependent on others [9]. For example, at the age of three autistic children may be introduced to social environments with other children. The autistic child may become overwhelmed with the added complexity at this stage of development (a new environment of new people), which may mean they start to experience negative emotion. This obviously happens for children whose family don't know their loved one is autistic, and therefore some parents may mistake this as a form of regression. Also, autistic people may have difficulty expressing emotion or intention within their own Social Engagement System which may make social interactions even more difficult during these critical periods of social development. The explanation of an atypical myelinated Social Engagement System can start to help explain why most autistic children prefer not to engage in social play with others.

The work by Jaak Panksepp highlights humans have a neural circuit specific for play that help develop the skills needed for social flexibility and reciprocity. It is likely this neural circuit needs wired within a critical period (before the age of five years). If the neural circuit of play is not fully developed within this critical period, then the child will have difficulty with social interactions and social flexibility throughout their life [3]. This is discussed in more detail in chapter 11.

The Social Engagement System and Autism B Theory

A baby is born with some basic reflexes. One such reflex is the ability to suck a nipple while gazing between the proximity of the mother's eye and nipple. These early interactions shape and promote signals of safety (smiles, laughing, imitation of positive emotion, tonality, and pitch), becoming more strengthened within the brain by oxytocin, serotonin and dopamine. It is likely this automated reflex is the beginning of developing the neural Social Engagement System [10].

The ability to laugh, smile, imitate, express emotion on the face, hear tonality and use pitch within speech all require motor movement. As already discussed, if voluntary motor movement is already atypical with autistic babies [11], this may mean they will have difficulty wiring up the Social Engagement System. If the Social Engagement System is atypical, then this will result in atypical social development.

Social Engagement System areas	Potential difficulty if atypically developed
Facial muscles	Lack of ability to express a range of emotions through facial expressions. May also have difficulty understanding the facial expressions of other people. May have difficulty with emotional attunement, imitation and understanding the emotional state of others. Possibly contributes to overall alexithymia and prosopagnosia for some people.
Third ear muscle	Lack of ability to hear the emotional range of other voices and/or sounds. May have difficulty with pitch and tone. For example, speech could be monotopic. May have difficulty hearing range of emotion in others speech. Possibly contributes to overall alexithymia for some people.
Voice	Lack of ability to express a range of emotion and infliction in voice. For example, may have monotone, very flat and/or robotic speech. Possibly contributes to overall alexithymia for some people.

If the brain can't read the social signals of other people in the environment, then the brain will eventually perceive the lack of social signals as an anomaly. An anomaly is an unknown. Eventually the brain will treat the unknown social signals as a threat. This is because the brain is primed for negative emotion before positive. It is better for the brain to be cautious around people rather than trusting, especially if the brain has difficulty reading the social signals of people. This can explain why social interactions are often very difficult for some autistic people.

Social interactions coupled with sensory sensitivities will often overload the autistic brain, resulting in neuroception (sometimes referred to as neural pain) [1]. Environments such as nurseries, school, college, university, work, supermarkets and social gatherings can therefore be overwhelming.

Neuroception will activate the fight, flight or freeze responses. When activated, the brain starts the process of shutting down the gut processes. There is a higher prevalence of autistic people with gut related issues (autoimmune challenges). Could it be that the difficulty understanding social signals is contributing to the shutdown of gut processes for autistic people, putting them at a higher risk of poor autoimmune health?

Also, autistic people may already have poor gut health issues as a result of low levels of B vitamins during their early development. If someone does have poor gut health, then this will also contribute to shutting down the positive system of the Social Engagement System needed to project and/or perceive smiles, soft tone and positive body language. If the positive side of the Social Engagement System is shut down, this then by default activates the fight, flight or freeze responses which include catatonia and situational mutism which negatively impacts gut and autoimmune health.

Atypical development of cranial nerves

Autism B Theory hypothesises atypically myelinated neurons during early development may result in atypical development of other cranial nerves. The neurons involved with cranial nerves 1, 2 and 8 are made of sensory neurons. Cranial nerves 3, 4, 6, 11, and 12 are made of motor neurons. Cranial nerves 5, 7, 9, and 10 are mixed with both sensory and motor neurons.

	Cranial Nerve	Function	Atypical development if atypically myelinated
1	Olfactory	Smell.	Atypical sensory sensitivities.
2	Optic	Vision.	Atypical sensory sensitivities.
3	Oculomotor	Eye movement: pupil constriction.	The affected eye turns slightly outward and downward possibly resulting in double vision.
4	Trochlear	Eye movement: rotational.	If one of these nerves is damaged the muscles may become paralysed to varying degrees.

5	Trigeminal	Somatosensory information (touch, pain) from the face, head and muscles for chewing.	Potential difficulty will result in Trigeminal neuralgia which is intense facial pain and possible facial tics.
6	Abducens	Eye movement: lateral.	The affected eye cannot turn fully outward and may turn inward. Difficulty may result in in double vision, severe headache and temporary blurring of vision when people move their head suddenly. Moebius syndrome is defined as congenital facial palsy combined with abnormal ocular abduction, caused by abnormal development of the 6th and 7th cranial nerves.
7	Facial	Somatosensory information from ear, and controls muscles used in facial expression.	Difficulty expressing, and/or understanding the emotional intentions of self and others.
8	Vestibulocochlear	Hearing and balance.	Sensory sensitivities with hearing and balance. May be hard to locate where sound is coming from. May experience fragmentated perception. For example: TV, or words on pages may jumble and may impact on parts of facial integration.
9	Glossopharyngeal	Receives sensory information from the tonsils, the pharynx, the middle ear and the rest of the tongue.	Difficulty hearing pitch and tone in others speech, may even be difficult for the person to use pitch effectively resulting in monotone speech.
10	Vagus	Social Engagement System. Sensory, motor, and autonomic functions of viscera (glands, digestion and heart rate).	Possible social communication difficulties and over-activation of the fight, flight or freeze responses, including catatonia and situational mutism.
11	Spinal Accessory	Controls muscles used in head movement, shoulders and neck.	Slower processing of sensory motor neurons needed for the Social Engagement System.
12	Hypoglossal	Controls muscles of tongue for speech and food manipulation.	Potential paralysis, fasciculations (scalloped appearance of the tongue), and possible atrophy of the tongue muscles.

Each autistic person will be different. The potential variation of atypical myelination for some cranial nerve development will be different for each autistic person. This helps explain the vast spectrum of divergence seen within the autistic population.

Atypical myelination of any of the cranial nerves will likely create difficulty in either the expressive or receptive skills needed for social interactions and understanding emotional intention. Such difficulty will impact on sensitive and critical periods, often resulting in atypical development.

References

1. Porges, Stephen W. The Polyvagal Theory: Neurophysiological Foundations of Emotions, Attachment, Communication, and Self-Regulation. Norton, 2011.
2. Lakna. "Difference between Nerve and Neuron: Definition, Types, Functions." Pediaa.Com, 13 July 2017, https://pediaa.com/difference-between-nerve-and-neuron/.
3. Panksepp, Jaak. Affective Neuroscience: The Foundations of Human and Animal Emotions. Oxford University Press, 2014.
4. Schmithorst, V. J., Holland, S. K., & Dardzinski, B. J. (2008). Developmental differences in white matter architecture between boys and girls. Human brain mapping, 29(6), 696–710. https://doi.org/10.1002/hbm.20431
5. Li WW, Penderis J, Zhao C, Schumacher M, Franklin RJ. Females remyelinate more efficiently than males following demyelination in the aged but not young adult CNS. Exp Neurol. 2006 Nov;202(1):250-4. doi: 10.1016/j.expneurol.2006.05.012. Epub 2006 Jun 22. PMID: 16797535.
6. Breton, J. M., Long, K., Barraza, M. K., Perloff, O. S., & Kaufer, D. (2021). Hormonal Regulation of Oligodendrogenesis II: Implications for Myelin Repair. Biomolecules, 11(2), 290. https://doi.org/10.3390/biom11020290
7. "Jordan Peterson – How to Properly Socialize Children." YouTube, YouTube, 19 Feb. 2019, https://www.youtube.com/watch?v=FXwZtg85zgU.
8. Empathy, Play and the Social Regulation of Aggression – Jordan Peterson. https://www.jordanbpeterson.com/

docs/230/2014/19Petersonplay.pdf. https://www.scholastic.
com/parents/family-life/social-emotional-learning/development-
milestones/social-development-3-5-year-olds.html

9. Carr, Alan. The Handbook of Child and Adolescent Clinical
Psychology: A Contextual Approach. Routledge, 2013.

10. Durkin, Kevin. Developmental Social Psychology: From Infancy to
Old Age. Wiley-Blackwell, 2012.

11. Torres, E. and Whyatt, C., 2018. Autism: The movement-sensing
perspective. 1st ed. Boca Raton : CRC Press, Taylor & Francis
Group, (2018)

Chapter 10
Emotional regulation and development

The most critical stage of emotional development seems to be between the age of two and three years.

In his book *Affective Neuroscience* [1], Jaak Panksepp identifies seven emotional systems that all humans have. The interaction of these emotional systems explains the variation of all human emotion.

Figure 12: Panksepp seven emotional systems.

Emotional system (Panksepp Affective Neuroscience)						
Seeking	**Play**	**Fear**	**Grief/Panic**	**Rage**	**Lust**	**Care**
Motivated, arousal, interested to seek change, curious	Joy, glee, happy, socially engaging, laughter, sense of humour	Anxiety, phobias, panic, trauma, worry	Separation distress, sadness, guilt, shame, embarrassment, poor-self image	Anger, irritability, rage	Erotic feelings, attraction	Nurturance, care, love

At the age of two it seems as if all the seven emotions are trying to take control, hence why this stage is often referred to as the Terrible Twos. This is because a baby can be curious, playful, fearful, upset, angry and happy all within a very small period of time. The ability to regulate these emotions during this critical period lays the foundation for future emotional regulation which helps the baby move onto the next stage of development.

Figure 10: Stages of development.

Stages of development
Sensory motor: 0-2 years.
Social emotional: 2-3 years.
Social development with others: 3-5 years.

Children usually start to play with other children around the age of three. At two, children can play by themselves but not so much with other children. This is partly because they are still developing their internal emotions. For example, children will only play with other children whose emotions can be easily understood. Understanding the emotion helps anticipate the behavioural intentions of others better. This helps children invite, connect and play with other children. For obvious reasons, children will not invite others to play if their emotions are unpredictable.

Emotional feelings arise from physiological changes within the body. This is why emotional regulation comes after the sensory motor development (embodiment). There needs to be a certain amount of sensory body awareness for the person to understand the bodily (physiological) representation of emotions. Internal sensations, feelings and awareness of what is happening inside the body is called interoception.

Interoception is the internal body signalling of things such as thirst, pain, hunger, toilet needs and emotional feelings. Interoception neurons rely on sensory, motor and interneurons to send signals to the brain about what is happening within the body. Atypical myelination of motor neurons may make it difficult for the brain to fully integrate all the sensory information needed to understand interoceptive needs. A person needs a fully developed motor system (proprioceptive sense) to be able to feel all the affective emotions in real time. An atypically sensory motor system will inevitably result in atypical emotional regulation. For example, some autistic people might explain they have difficulty understanding their emotional feelings. Often autistic people may say things like *"It is too difficult to explain emotions using words."* If the feelings and emotions have been developed atypically, then of course some autistic people will have difficulty using typical emotional language to describe their atypical emotional experiences and feelings; they have a different bodily experience for all the range of emotions compared to neurotypical people. This can often mean therapeutic supports may be difficult to engage with initially. If the therapy or therapist doesn't acknowledge the autistic person may have difficulty using typical emotional words to describe their atypical emotional experiences, then the therapy may fail before it has even started. This can help explain why some autistic people create words to express how they feel.

If autistic people have difficulty with their interoception and proprioception senses, it will likely result in difficulty understanding and controlling emotional regulation. This helps explain why you may hear some autistic people say things like their emotions are escaping out their body, or they are not sure whose emotions they are experiencing as they don't know where their emotions end and someone else's begin [2]. This is why people will often move or stim when trying to process emotions; the movement helps the body identify the bodily emotional effect and feeling. Poor emotional regulation can also be explained by alexithymia (this is when a person has difficulty identifying and expressing emotions). Alexithymia is discussed in more detail in Appendix 4.

If autistic people have difficulty understanding emotional feelings, then this likely impact on the next stage of development: social play with other children. In order to play with others, children need to have an understanding of their own emotional intent and that of others. Atypical emotional regulation, coupled with sensory sensitivities and potential difficulty reading the social and emotional intentions of others (atypical Social Engagement System), could mean play with others is too difficult. Instead, the autistic child will prefer to play alone, being more interested in things rather than people.

References

1. Panksepp, Jaak. Affective Neuroscience: The Foundations of Human and Animal Emotions. Oxford University Press, 2014.
2. Bennie, Maureen, et al. "Interoception and Autism : Body Awareness Challenges for Those with ASD." Autism Awareness, 23 May 2022, https://autismawarenesscentre.com/interoception-and-autism-body-awareness-challenges-for-those-with-asd/.

Chapter 11
Social development

There is a neural system for play that starts developing as soon as the baby is born [1]. For example, activities like peekaboo, breastfeeding, smiling, laughing and tickling are all play-like interactions. This is why play is the beginning of social development.

Play is essentially a set of predictable behaviours. You can only play with another when you both agree to act within certain expectations (rules) of that social space for a specific period of time. For obvious reasons, if someone doesn't play by the rules then people will no longer want to play with that person. For example, if a baby smiles but nobody smiles back, the baby will stop engaging in the smiling game. Play is the foundation for all future reciprocal social interactions [2].

An important element needed for play is the ability to anticipate what others will do. This is partly achieved through the support of mirror neurons. These neurons are some of the first to be myelinated at birth. There is still some uncertainty about the specific role of mirror neurons, but there is a general consensus that these neurons are needed to imitate and understand both body language and facial expressions.

A mirror neuron can also be described as a visuospatial neuron. This is because mirror neurons are activated when the person sees someone else performing an action. The visuospatial neurons mirrors the action (behaviour) of others as though the observer themselves was acting out the same action they are observing. This is why these neurons help develop imitation, play, empathy, learning new skills and various others. This is likely why mirror neurons play a crucial role during sensitive and critical periods of social development.

Research from the Washington and Temple University [3] has highlighted how observation supports imitation during development. The research demonstrates when babies are watching other people, their mirror neurons are mapping the movement of others onto their own body. This process of observation helps the baby develop sensory and body awareness.

Babies learn from the sensory motor system up. The baby embodies the actions and movements of others with the support of mirror neurons. Babies observe how other people do things and eventually they start to copy those body movements themselves. Babies first imitate their caregiver's voices, sounds, actions and then gestures. Eventually toddlers interact by copying each other's actions with increasing complexity throughout childhood, helping develop more sophisticated social skills. Imitation is how children learn pre-verbally, becoming more complex as the child grows and develops.

Figure 11: Cognitive development from sensory motor movement upwards.

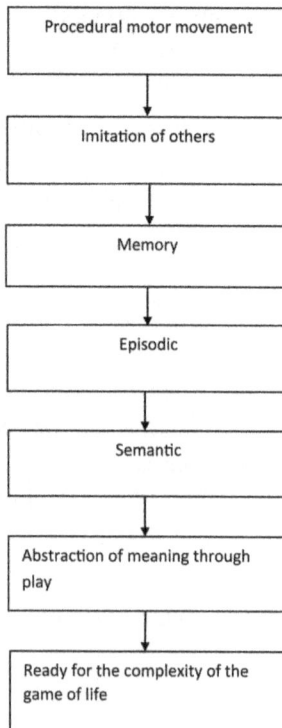

Over time memory can start to make sense of this embodied knowledge, which then develops episodic memory. Eventually the baby starts to associate the embodied knowledge with specific words which then allows them to start talking (semantics). Talking then supports mental thought and abstraction for more complex learning, eventually helping the person prepare for more complex social interactions. Figure 11 highlights this process [2].

Mirror neurons enable a person to mentally simulate not just other people's actions, but the intentions and emotions behind those actions. This is sometimes explained as theory of mind. Such embodiment of another's perspective helps develop an idea of what the other person may be doing or experiencing. This gives the observer the possibility of having a shared understanding of the behaviours and intentions of others in that shared social space. For example, when a person sees someone smile, mirror neurons in the observer's brain activate too, creating a sensation in the observers own mind of the feelings associated with smiling. The same could be said for observing any human action. This explains why mirror neurons help people enjoy TV, theatre, sports and movies. The mirror neurons give the observer a sense of what the actor is doing or experiencing, gripping their attention and emotional experience. If the mirror neuron system is not fully developed for an autistic person (or is atypical), then this will likely impact on the person's ability to infer what others are doing in the same shared social space.

The neural explanation for social and emotional awareness (sometimes conflated with empathy) cannot be fully explained by mirror neurons alone. However, atypically myelinated mirror neurons, (coupled with sensory sensitivities and atypically myelinated Social Engagement Neurons) can start to explain why so many autistic people struggle with various elements of social interactions.

There has been debate over how much mirror neurons can explain the autistic disposition. Some research has demonstrated that mirror neurons do work for autistic people, they just run slower [4, 5, 6]. Other research explains mirror neurons play a more substantial role within the autistic brain. Autism B Theory can bridge these different perspectives.

It is likely that atypical myelination may result in some people's mirror neurons being atypical. Other autistic people may not have had any difficulty with the myelination of the mirror neurons but may have had difficulty with the myelination of sensory motor neurons, or cranial nerve neurons needed for other aspects of social interactions [7]. The difference with how much and when atypical myelination takes place for different neurons will be due to multiple factors such as genetics, the biological demand of pregnancy, as well as the various other causes related to autism. This is why there hasn't been a clear consensus on the exact role of mirror neurons within autism in relation to social development.

Play, social rules, norms and expectations

Autistic people are more nervous and self-conscious in social situations when compared with the majority of neurotypical people. For example, the difficulty in understanding the social and emotional intentions of others will often result in the autistic person becoming emotional, self-conscious and ultimately afraid when engaged in some sort of social interaction, particularly with strangers.

An approach by a stranger starts the process of anxiety and panic. It is therefore helpful to determine if the stranger is a possible threat. This is why small talk can be useful. Small talk helps determine the emotional stability of the stranger. This is mainly why neurotypical people engage in it.

For example, at a bus stop one may observe small talk such as *"How are you? … some weather today?"* When engaged in this small talk people are generally not intending to ask those questions literally, instead the questions are intended to look for people who will or will not behave by the social rules that appear to govern most social interactions. It is as if by engaging in small talk the brain is determining *"is the person going to violate the expectation of this social domain at a bus stop, are they therefore dangerous?"* If the other person replies to the small talk with, *"I'm fine thanks … yeah nice weather … nice to see you too"*, then they are unconsciously signalling that they will abide by the social rules of bus stop behaviour. This then signals that there may be an opportunity to develop a connection and additional social talk may follow.

If a person was not to abide by the social rules of bus stop behaviour (for example shouting or not answering back), then people in that area will unconsciously develop the opinion that the person's behaviour cannot be predicted and they are therefore to be treated with suspicion. This starts the effect of negative emotion (threat, panic, anxiety).

If social interactions are play like then we can infer those interactions have to follow expectations. For example, a board game can only work if people agree to the expectations of how to act within that social space when playing that board game, if people don't the game falls into chaos. The exact same could be said for the mini games of social interactions such as small talk. If people don't behave within an agreed set of expectations then social order will collapse. The difficulty autistic people have is that social order is mainly neurotypical. However, there are potentially biological reasons that may explain why neurotypical people behave the way they do (explained below).

The neural system for developing unconscious social skills

The neuroscientist Jaak Panksepp identified the neural system for play. Panksepp demonstrated that mammals (including humans) need to play to help their physical and social development. Panksepp discovered that when smaller juvenile rats were repeatedly paired with bigger older rats to play (dummy fighting), the bigger rats would let the smaller rats win 30% of the time [1]. Panksepp discovered the older rats were teaching the younger rats the social skills of reciprocity and flexibility during critical periods of development. Such learning at this critical period helped the younger rats become successful during future social interactions with other rats. Such opportunities to play during critical periods of development matures the neural networks for mammals (including humans) to be socially flexible with up to 30% change before experiencing emotional distress.

Panksepp established that all mammals act out a neuro system (the play system) that helps develop social skills of reciprocity and flexibility. For humans, it is likely this critical period of unconsciously learning social reciprocity and flexibility is done before the age of five years, but only if their development has been typical.

The development of social skills is complex neurology. This is why it has been very difficult to create socially aware automated machines. If artificial intelligence has difficulty computing social situations, then this demonstrates how hard it is for autistic people to learn social skills consciously. If the child has not developed the neural network of play by the age of 5 years then the child will have social difficulties throughout their lives [1].

It could be argued that the play system evolved to promote altruistic behaviours. Panksepp's work (the discovery of the neuro play system) can explain why neurotypical people are comfortable with social flexibility and change of 30% before they start to experience negative emotion. Panksepp's work demonstrated that play takes children to their emotional edge, therefore meaning they are unconsciously learning the balance of being flexible with others up to 30% of the time while also having the opportunity to have their own needs and wishes met [1].

This can help explain why there are no set strict rules of social interactions. Rules would stagnate the flexibility needed for positive creativity that affords new and exciting opportunities for people and communities to grow and develop.

The unconscious ability of at least 30% flexibility means neurotypical people have the potential to make changes that are in their best interests, but so long as they accommodate the changes made or requested by other people within society. Such flexibility allows both individuals and societies to progress together. This behaviour can be described as altruistic morality: engaging with what is good for the greater society while also benefiting yourself. It is as if society tolerates some flexibility but not when others constantly try and benefit themselves without making any sacrifice to the wider group. However, there can't be too much change, there needs to be some sort of balance. This is why the tolerance of change is roughly 30% across the neurotypical population. Unfortunately, some people do take advantage of the flexible nature of others, with these people being labelled as selfish and greedy

A good guide to understand neurotypical behaviour is to assume that a neurotypical person will be able to roughly deal with at least 30% of change before they start to experience negative emotion. This can partly explain why neurotypical people can cope with not sticking to exact dates or times, being late, updating or changing plans, going with the flow, be willing to allow a certain degree of change, be tolerant of other people's white lies and various other examples of social fluidity.

The work of Panksepp and ethos of altruism can be closely linked to Jean Piaget's model of social development [2]. Piaget believed play and games helped develop a sense of morality (altruism) for development. Play is essentially preparing the young person for the game of adult life [2]. Piaget believed there are three types of games that help shape development. These are: win/lose games, cooperative games and equilibrated games (the highest morality of games) [2]. This is because equilibrated games are when everyone can participate and benefit at the same time; everyone cooperates and nobody loses. Such games are essentially altruistic by nature.

The combined factors of a young autistic person's atypical development (sensory sensitivities, atypical emotional regulation, atypical Social Engagement System and potentially atypical mirror neuron development) will ultimately mean the autistic person will not have the opportunity to unconsciously learn the social flexibility within the critical period before the age of 5 years.

Perceived rules, social flexibility and cooperation

Generally speaking, autistic people struggle with the flexible nature of social interactions and change. Having rules and structure in place makes people and organisations predictable. It is often the unclear, unclarified, unknown and anything ambiguous that creates anxiety.

Autistic people often struggle to understand the unwritten rules that govern social behaviour, and as a result society has tried to teach autistic people what are the social rules through things like social skills training. By following the rules one can usually predict what will happen. However, this is often very difficult because the taught rules of social skills are not always applicable and change with context. For example, someone may have been taught, *"always ask permission to use someone's toilet"*. Then, when at a restaurant the autistic person sees someone entering the toilet without asking for permission. This confuses the autistic person because they are observing someone else not following the rules of using the toilet as has been taught to them. They then tell the person who used the toilet *"you are not following the toilet rules"*, which results in an argument (the autistic person has not understood the context of being in a restaurant means it is okay to use the toilet without permission so long as they [or someone with them] are a customer).

The underlying meaning of the word rules is the perception that they must not be broken, yet people disregard rules all the time. Rules are usually taught in a way which describes how people will generally act in a certain situation, so autistic people follow them believing everyone else will too but become frustrated when others stop following the rules as has been taught or explained.

Autistic people often develop a high sense of integrity and morality. The autistic person will often follow the rules but will feel deflated or annoyed when others don't. Some autistic people can often develop insightful meta ideas about social behaviour within disciplines such as ethics, psychology, sociology and philosophy but struggle to make sense of human behaviour at the micro level for things such as being late, white lies and people not doing exactly what they said they would.

This isn't to say neurotypical people don't value integrity of perceived social rules, they do, but they also unconsciously value flexibility because they know that life is too complex for one set of rules to govern all social interactions.

This is why teaching social rules often results in difficulty for autistic people. Life is too complex for one set of rules to describe and maintain social order. Societal interactions (apart from the law) do not work on a set of rules, they work on a set of principles. The main principle is cooperation, with the highest ideal being altruism. Therefore, the learning for autistic people shouldn't be about rules, it should be about the underlying principle which helps shape social behaviour.

Hopefully this chapter has helped explain why some autistic people think neurotypical people can be shifty, socially manipulative, rule breaking, unreliable and potentially untrustworthy. However, as autistic people are often insistent on structure, rules and fairness, can explain why neurotypical people often think autistic people can be rigid, intolerant and inflexible. Hopefully a better understanding of both autistic and neurotypical social development can help develop a greater appreciation of each other. An explanation of the different thinking styles of autistic and neurotypical people is further explained in chapter 13.

References

1. Panksepp, Jaak, et al. "Chapter 9." The Archaeology of Mind: Neuroevolutionary Origins of Human Emotions, W. W Norton, New York, 2012.
2. J Peterson, Jordan B. "Chapter 2." Maps of Meaning, Taylor and Francis, S.I., 2002.
3. "A First Step in Learning by Imitation, Baby Brains Respond to Another's Actions." UW News, https://www.washington.edu/news/2013/10/30/a-first-step-in-learning-by-imitation-baby-brains-respond-to-anothers-actions/.
4. Dinstein, Ilan, et al. "Normal Movement Selectivity in Autism." Neuron, vol. 66, no. 3, 2010, pp. 461–469., https://doi.org/10.1016/j.neuron.2010.03.034
5. "'Broken Mirror' Concept of Autism Challenged: Spectrum: Autism Research News." Spectrum, 3 Mar. 2011, https://www.spectrumnews.org/news/broken-mirror-concept-of-autism-challenged/.

6. "'Broken Mirror' Concept of Autism Challenged: Spectrum: Autism Research News." Spectrum, 3 Mar. 2011, https://www.spectrumnews. org/news/broken-mirror-concept-of-autism-challenged/.

7. Chan, M.M.Y., Han, Y.M.Y. Differential mirror neuron system (MNS) activation during action observation with and without social-emotional components in autism: a meta-analysis of neuroimaging studies. Molecular Autism 11, 72 (2020). https://doi.org/10.1186/ s13229-020-00374-x Sdjhchjsdb

Chapter 12

Autism B Theory, executive function skills, perception, change and the non-literal meaning of words.

Autism B Theory suggests autistic people may have difficulty with executive functioning skills as a consequence of atypical sensory motor development [1].

Executive function skills consist of planning ahead, problem-solving, working memory, time management, organisational skills and self-control. Even thinking about doing something uses executive function skills.

When people think about doing something they use the motor-action areas of the brain [2]. Thinking activates the sensory motor neurons to mentally simulate (imagine) what potential movements may be needed to undertake the thought or idea. The motor-action areas of the brain are heavily involved in executive functions skills.

Unconscious brain processes needed for executive function skills

Most people have a limited understanding of how human visual perception works. The general consensus is that people see objects and this helps them become conscious of what is in the environment. This is technically wrong. This is because there are simply too many objects in the visual field for the brain to consciously process. For example, when someone is observing a nature park, they are not consciously aware of the exact number of trees, never mind the number of leaves on each tree; there is simply too much detail for the brain to consciously perceive. If the brain did consciously process all the objects in the environment it would be overwhelmed. Instead, the brain classifies visual information into categories of objects rather than process the intrinsic qualities of each object. This allows the brain to focus its energy on what is important at any given time. Eventually, it is only the important things that people become consciously aware of. This means there must be initial unconscious processes in the brain that informs conscious awareness of what may be important [3]. Some autistic people explain they often have difficulty filtering out all the details in the environment, making it difficult to filter out what is important and what is not [4].

The brain helps determine what is important (in the environment), by filtering what has been perceived through motor areas. This means that the motor area, and ultimately motor neurons, influences conscious perception. It is as if the brain asks the motor area if it has the potential muscle movement to engage with the things it has seen in the environment. Gibson described these unconscious brain processes as affordances [5].

It is as if the brain needs support from the motor area to determine what the objects in environment can afford the person, for example, is there affordances of threats or opportunities in the visual field? Affordances of opportunities could be observing there are seats to sit on, a cup to drink from, a pen to pick up, a tree stump to sit on, a fountain to drink from and so on. Affordances of threat could be a cliff to fall from, a hole to fall into, a tree branch to stumble over and so on.

The possibility of opportunity or threat can only be determined by how well the person can interact (through the activation of motor neurons) with the things or objects seen in the environment. The motor area can activate an arrangement of motor neurons to take advantage of affordances or avoid threats [6].

The brain stores information about the body, as well as information about the environment and integrates them. This combined knowledge helps the brain perceive how the body can interact with the external world, or take advantage or avoid affordances [7].

Figure 15: Executive function brain and sensory motor areas.

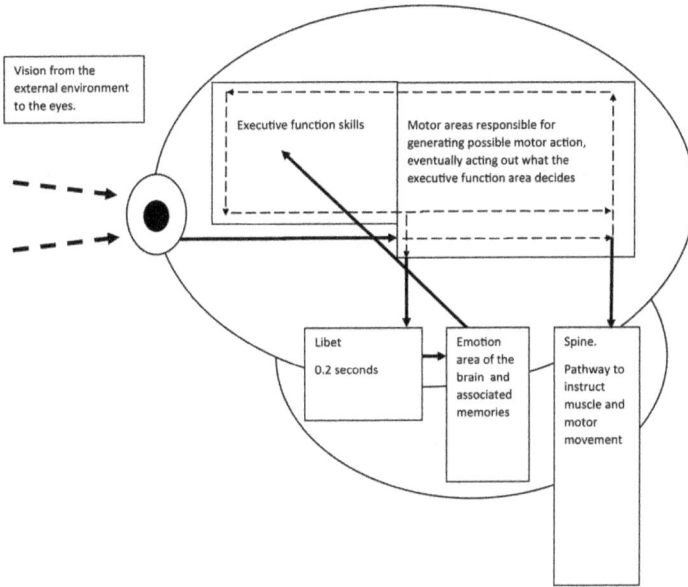

For example, a person may be looking at a field which has a tree stump. Their brain then perceives the tree stump as the affordance of a makeshift seat, not just a tree stump. This is because the brain has used the motor area to determine how the body could interact with the environment. As the body has the muscle memory of how to sit, the motor area informs the executive function area that there is potential muscle ability to sit by the affordance of the tree stump in the environment, this is when the person becomes consciously aware of the tree stump as the affordance of a sitting opportunity. Such awareness of affordances usually happens within 0.2 seconds. This means that all the sensory information from the environment is unconsciously perceived, integrated, and organised for human consciousness through the motor areas within at least 0.2 seconds [8].

This hopefully explains how vision and perception are strongly linked to motor neurons. You see with your eyes, but you also perceive the environment with motor neurons before being consciously aware of how to possibly act.

If the brain can't figure out what motor movement is needed to deal with objects or threats in the environment after 0.2 seconds, it will slowly start to activate the anxiety and panic systems. It does this because from an evolutionary perspective 0.2 seconds is a long time when exposed to a potential threat. This helps explain why the brain will scan the environment for any danger or anomaly before opportunity. You will have experienced this yourself. When walking into a room you have been in countless times before, your brain will notice anything unusual such as new furniture. The new furniture is an anomaly because it forces the brain to think about formulating new motor patterns of behaviour to deal with the change. The same could be said if there was a change to the layout of the furniture. This is because it takes time for the brain to think and adjust to all the potential new muscle patterns of behaviour (new arrangement of motor neurons) to successfully navigate the change [9]. If the brain can't prepare the motor movement needed to deal with the anomaly within 0.2 seconds, then as each 0.2 seconds pass, the brain will start to become anxious.

Here is an example, say there is a very small dog perceived in the environment. The brain will access the motor areas to determine if there is potential motor ability to handle such a small dog. This is done by preparing and pooling all the motor neurons needed to perform actions of safely handling a small dog. Such pooling of neurons informs the brain that there is the potential motor ability to deal with a small dog. This allows the brain to use executive functioning skills to interact with the dog if needed, all within 0.2 seconds. Say there is another dog, but this time a bigger dog. The same brain process occurs. However, the motor area may not be able to generate the potential motor neuron pool needed to handle this bigger dog. The motor area informs the executive function area that there is no potential motor neuron pool to deal with a dog this size. This then limits the brain's ability to think of how to safely interact with the bigger dog (reduction of executive function ability), therefore making the person anxious and apprehensive about the possible dangers of not knowing what to do. The fight, flight or freeze responses may eventually be activated. As you can see, it is the person's potential motor ability that initially starts to determine the risk of danger before other aspects are considered. The motor area of the brain initially informs what is possible for the executive functioning area to act out.

The closer the object(s), including other people, the more the brain relies on the motor areas for perception [7]. The brain does this by calculating the peripersonal space in relation to what is perceived in the environment. The peripersonal space is the space surrounding the body where a person can voluntarily reach out and interact with objects and people. The peripersonal space is dependent on proprioception receptors. It is well documented that autistic people struggle with their peripersonal space (proprioception under sensitivity).

Here is an example of how the peripersonal space influences perception and executive function skills. Say a person enters a room that has a chair, a cup, a pen and a light switch. Unconsciously the motor area of the brain will run the potential motor ability (generate potential motor neuron pools) needed to sit on the chair, hold the cup, pick up the pen and flick the switch, all within 0.2 seconds. This allows the person to become consciously aware of their executive function skills of how to interact with objects in the environment.

This is why rooms, or environments that have a lot of objects in them are described as busy (even though the objects are not moving). Additional objects in the environment places more demand on the motor areas to map out all the potential motor movements needed to potentially interact with all the objects, hence why perceiving such environments feels busy (the motor area is working at a busy rate). Obviously, autistic people use more mental energy for perception as a result of their under sensitive motor system. This is why clutter free environments can be effective for some autistic people as it prevents them from using unnecessary mental energy. This doesn't mean environments have to be sterile, instead, environments should be functional and intuitive.

What are muscle generator pools?

A muscle generator pool is a number of motor neurons that are pooled together to perform a specific muscle movement. The eventual muscle movement is then perceived behaviour [9]. Small pools of neurons are needed for minor movements, and larger pools for bigger movements. For example, there is a generator pool of motor neurons for each finger to flex, which is nested in a bigger pool for the hand to move and so on. More complex actions require multiple neuron pools. For example social interactions requires constant changing of neuron pools to socially engage with others due to the animate and dynamic behaviour of people. Mostly all the neurons in these pools are myelinated as this helps speed up executive functioning ability.

Figure 16: Example of a muscle motor generator pool.

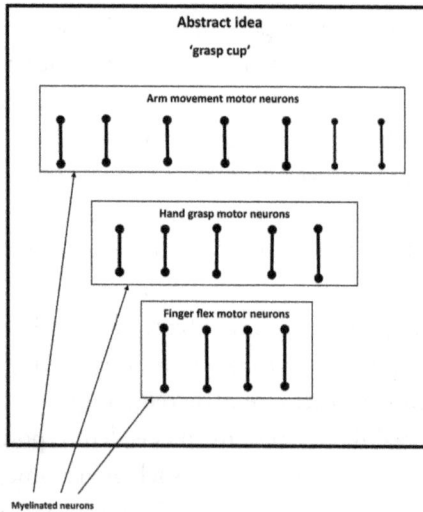

Figure 17: a myelinated neuron

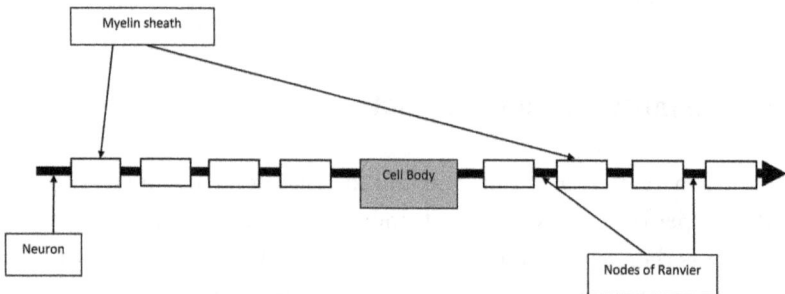

The thick white boxes are the layers of myelin sheath, enabling fast and precise communication with neighbouring neurons.

Figure 18: an atypical myelinated neuron

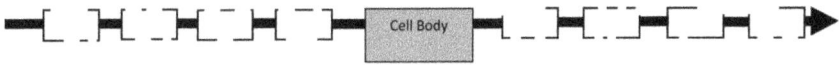

The myelin sheath in Figure 18 is atypically myelinated, resulting in slower communication with neighbouring neurons. The slowing down of communication will likely impact on the brains ability to determine what to do within 0.2 seconds.

Figure 19: Comparison of different myelinated neuron pools.

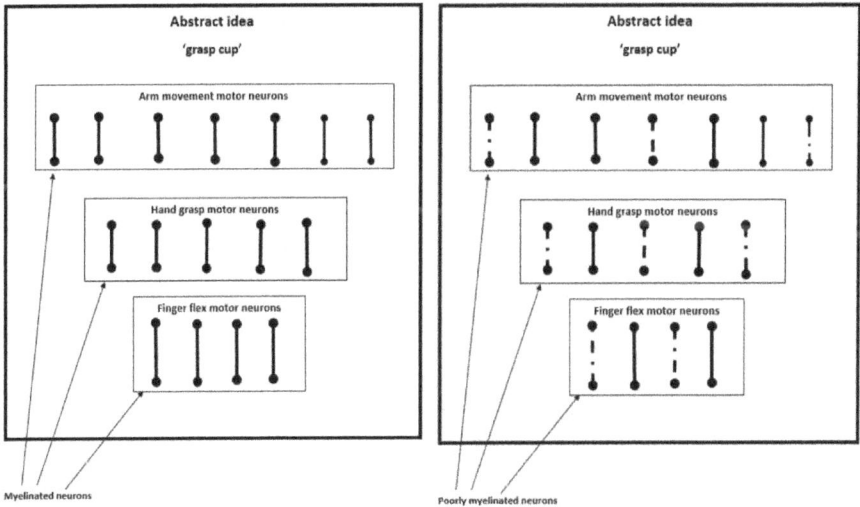

Autism B Theory, executive function skills, perception and change

Autism B Theory proposes that atypically myelinated neurons in early development may mean autistic people could experience difficulties with executive functioning skills and change throughout their life. This can explain why autistic people struggle with changes, house moves, new furniture, new workplaces, different travel routes and new people. It can also lead to difficulty with smaller changes and demands such as housework, dishes, clutter, letters and putting away belongings.

Any change means the person needs to react differently which requires a different arrangement of motor neuron pools. The difficulty autistic people have is that their motor area will sometimes take longer than 0.2 seconds to arrange new pools.

The reason why there is only 0.2 seconds is hard to explain, however, understanding how the brain evolved can help. For simplicity, the brain can be hypothetically arranged into two parts: the bottom part of the brain being the old brain, and the newer evolved part of the brain (the prefrontal cortex) that grew on top of this ancient brain.

The prefrontal cortex is where the executive function skills are located. Executive function skills are problem solving, planning ahead, motivation, imagination and attention. Such skills have helped humans evolve into the dominant species that has transformed the world. Before the prefrontal cortex evolved, it was the old brain that had all the control. Through evolution, the old brain was so impressed with the skills of the newly evolved prefrontal cortex it agreed to hand over voluntary control to it. However, the old brain stated if the new executive function area becomes complacent, hesitant, or puts the body in potential danger, then it will take control back briefly. A deal was done. Essentially, the old brain only allows the executive function area 0.2 seconds to decide what to do. If for any reason the executive function area cannot decide what to do in 0.2 seconds, then the old brain starts to take control back, assuming more control as each 0.2 seconds pass.

The problem for autistic people is that the delay in activating motor generated neuron pools is often due to atypically myelinated neurons. Even if there is only a limited period of atypical myelination during early development, it may still be enough to create difficulty, delay or hesitation within the motor neuron pools needed for executive functioning skills throughout life.

Unfortunately for the autistic brain, the old brain does not understand the delay in activating the muscle generator pools needed for executive skills is because of atypically myelinated neurons. Instead, the old brain only perceives the delay as a signal that the executive function area does not know how to act. As each 0.2 seconds passes the more the old brain starts to take control back, eventually resulting in panic and anxiety which further impacts on the executive function area to think clearly. Eventually the old brain will instruct the executive function area to stop thinking of doing anything new, forcing the executive function area to resort back to behaviours that are safe. This can help explain why autistic people often fall back into the previous way of doing things when stressed or anxious.

If there are no additional pressures for the autistic brain, then it may be able to fully utilise executive function skills. However, if there are additional pressures such as sensory sensitivities, social communication barriers and previous traumatic experiences, then this will temporarily impact on executive function ability, explaining why, at times, some autistic people become resistant to change or anything that makes them think about change.

Supports such as visual supports, verb instructions, mirroring actions, role play, social stories, now & next cards, timetables and various other supports can all help autistic people anticipate change better.

Autonoetic consciousness

The brain has the amazing ability of mental future time travel to help predict what may unfold in the future [10]. This ability is called autonoetic consciousness. It has had a huge evolutionary advantage for humans. This obviously means that people can avoid dangerous situations as they have thought of a less dangerous alternative action to take. This helps people keep safe while seeking better opportunities. However, trying to imagine what future changes may be like is very difficult for a lot of autistic people.

The brain uses the executive function part of the prefrontal cortex when planning what to do in the present and future. The prefrontal cortex developed from older evolutionary motor systems. This helped develop the ability for exploration, including mental exploration (thinking without movement) [11]. For example, the created thought of potential action (a set of generated motor neuron pools) is then sent to the motor area to act out at a later date when needed [13, 14 and 15]. This highlights to even think requires the use of motor areas of the brain [12].

Atypically myelinated neurons may prevent the autistic person acting out their mental plan, and therefore the person may revert back to previous patterns of behaviour. Such experiences often creates a lot of inner personal conflict for the autistic person as they know what can be done but often have great difficulty putting it into action. This eventually results in low mood and poor self-esteem.

Autistic executive function processing model

The autistic executive function processing model in Figure 20 is heavily influenced by the work of Jeffrey Gray [16]. The model explains how motor neurons can influence executive functioning skills for autistic people. There is a more detailed description of the associated brain functions in Appendix 6.

Figure 20: Executive function processing model

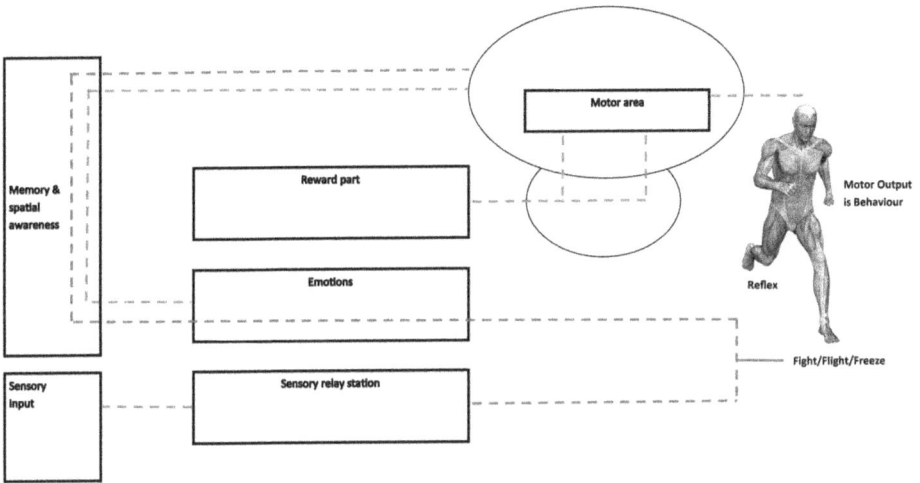

Memory & spatial awareness	Reward part
Sensory Input	Emotions
	Sensory relay station

Motor area

Motor Output is Behaviour

Reflex

Fight/Flight/Freeze

All sensory input is sent to the sensory relay station in the brain. The relay station then sends the information to the most appropriate parts of the brain. If the sensory information is perceived as an imminent threat, say a loud noise, the relay station will activate the fight, flight or freeze responses.

If the incoming sensory information is not an imminent threat, the relay station will do a few things at once. It will access the memory and spatial awareness systems to ask if there are any associated memories relevant to the incoming sensory information as this may help the brain understand how best to respond.

The relay station then informs the emotions part of the brain about the information and associated memories. It is as if the brain is asking itself *"Should we be happy, angry or sad about this incoming sensory information?"* The emotional systems then activate feelings based on previous experiences. It is as if the emotional systems determine, *"This is good… this is bad… this is scary"*. Again, all this happens unconsciously within 0.2 seconds. This awareness helps executive functioning skills decide what to do with the incoming sensory information.

The executive function area will then work with the motor area of the brain to try and decide what to do. It is as if it is asking, *"What would be the best arrangement of motor neuron pools to act on the incoming sensory information?"* If the motor area can generate a plan (a pool of potential motor neurons), then the reward part of the brain generates a small dopamine release and rewards the motor area. If the executive function area decides to act, it will instruct the motor area to carry out the action of the generated motor neuron pool. The action of motor neurons is then perceived behaviour.

If the plan can't go ahead, for whatever reason (atypical myelination patterns), then the brain goes back to the memory and spatial awareness areas asking if there is any additional information from similar experiences that could be used to make a new plan of what to do. The memory and spatial awareness part scans for previous memories associated with the stimuli. Mirror and sensory neurons are used to help imagine how previous memories could be manipulated to arrange a new mental story or idea of how to act. These new ideas are sent back down to the emotions part of the brain for the cycle to happen again, hopefully resulting in an updated plan of action being formulated, or in other words, a new set of pooled motor neurons generated to help undertake such action. Such a process will happen until a successful idea is thought and acted on. However, the longer this cycle continues (0.2 seconds), the more the old brain will start to take over executive functioning skills which may result in feelings of anxiety and panic.

Trying to understand other people

As discussed in previous chapters, the Social Engagement System and mirror neurons may be atypically myelinated, meaning the brain will be either slower, or at a disadvantage when processing the movement of other people. This means the autistic brain takes longer to activate the neurons needed for social interactions (0.2 seconds). This makes it very difficult for the autistic brain to use executive function skills socially, particularly in neurotypical environments.

Why is it that some autistic people display excellent executive function skills with some things but can be poor in others? For example, an autistic person may be utilising executive function skills with maths, engineering, physics, chemistry and biology, yet have poor skill with things such as opening mail, organising themselves or dealing with a small change of plan. The difference that explains this paradox is motor movement. When the brain is processing abstract ideas of math, engineering and science, it doesn't need to use motor and mirror neurons to visualise these in the mind's eye. As no sensory motor movement is needed (no need to try to visualise the movement of oneself or another), the brain can process these things without activating the 0.2 seconds threshold set by the old brain. This can explain why some autistic people gravitate towards such disciplines in education, natural interests and employment.

Some autistic people may be very intelligent but can often experience anxiety for things such as life admin. Letters, organising mail, money and planned meetings all put a demand on the person in the future. For example, a letter is usually a reminder that something is going to happen in the future. This means there needs to be a commitment of behaviour in the future (the need for future motor neurons to be pooled together). Even money puts ambiguous demands on the person in the future. For example, the autistic person may develop negative self-talk such as *"I'll have to spend that money at some point, what do I spend it on, what if it doesn't go to plan, do I need to interact with people, what if they ask questions, what if I can't decide what to do next?"* Eventually the person becomes too anxious with these ambiguous future scenarios because they can't develop the mental story in their head which would help the executive function skills problem solve for what could be done. This is why things such as social stories, visuals, event planning, scripting and visual story boards can help autistic people with planning ahead. Such supports help the person develop an understanding of possible future events which give more clarity. This doesn't mean autistic people cannot undertake executive function tasks. Instead, this explain why it can be difficult for some people, especially during times of stress and overload.

Difficulties with humour, sarcasm and non-literal use of language

Humour

Humour relies on timing. Essentially what makes a joke funny is the time it takes the brain to figure out the anomaly. The anomaly could be a contradiction, a violation of logic or something that doesn't initially make sense. Any anomaly causes the brain to be curious and anxious at the same time.

The story of the joke puts the expectation on the listener to solve the anomaly in the quickest time possible. If the person can problem solve the anomaly within 0.2 seconds, then the person finds the joke funny… they have understood the punchline as the saying goes. Any longer than 0.2 seconds and the punchline is often lost rendering the joke unfunny.

The reason why there is a time limit for a joke to be funny is related to the reward system highlighted within Figure 20. Basically, dopamine is what makes people feel good. The quicker the person can problem solve, the bigger the dopamine reward. From an evolutionary perspective, the people who could problem solve the quickest had better access to resources, so it makes sense that evolution would reward people with a dopamine release for quick problem-solving ability. The exact same reward process happens with a joke.

Most jokes indicate a social scene with at least one actor. For example, *"A person walks into a bar… Knock knock…"* This means the listener has to mentally project the story in their own head. Such mental visualisation requires the use of motor and mirror neurons to enable the person to visually generate the joke story in their head. Initially the joke doesn't make sense, so the brain needs to access memories associated with similar themes of the context of the joke as this helps the brain use imagery and imagination to figure out the anomaly. Generally speaking, within 0.2 seconds the person's memory will make the associated context and this enables the brain to figure out the anomaly of the joke; the punchline. As the person has solved the anomaly of the joke, the reward part of the brain releases a strong dopamine release, making the person feel good generating laughter. For example, a horse walks into a bar. The bar man asks, "*Why such a long face?*" It takes a bit of time to figure out the anomaly… why would a horse walk into a bar?… why would a man ask a horse a question?… why would the horse be so down it had to go into a bar? All this unconscious processing happens within 0.2 seconds. During this time the brain accesses the memory systems to look for context of horse faces, long and bar. Eventually the person mentally visualises that all horses have long faces compared to humans and this has nothing to do with needing a drink at a bar. As the anomaly is figured out within 0.2 seconds, dopamine is released and laughter follows. Obviously, atypical myelination of motor and mirror neurons will slow down the process of simulating the mental projection needed for the executive function skills to understand some jokes. This will often result in the punchline going past 0.2 seconds which therefore means the potential reward of dopamine is lost and the intended joke is not funny.

The delivery of a joke often requires the teller to use prosody and facial expression to emphasise important elements of the joke. If an autistic person has difficulty with detecting prosody and/or facial expressions (atypical myelination of the 7th cranial nerve), then this will further impact on their ability to understand the context of the joke.

This isn't to say autistic people do not find jokes or humour funny, of course autistic people have a sense of humour. The above scenario is just to explain why certain elements of humour may be difficult for some. For example, autistic people may experience a play on words more humorous as this does not place demand on motor and mirror neurons to mentally visualise the joke. Also, slapstick comedy may be humorous due to the delayed and obvious build up to the humour. Everyone will be different.

The same brain processes to understand jokes can also be used to understand why sarcasm and the non-literal use of words can be difficult for some autistic people.

Sarcasm

Sarcasm is an ironic or satirical remark which is intended to generate humour for those involved. The ironic statement is meant to create an anomaly, something to be figured out just like the punchline of a joke. Again, understanding sarcasm involves mental visualisation. If the listener can solve the anomaly quickly (0.2 seconds), they may find the sarcastic comment funny.

Situation	Sarcastic comments
Wet and rainy weather outside	"Great, the best dry day this year"
When something predictable happens	"WOW, who would have guessed that?"
When someone does something wrong	"Well done, that's a great job"
People that like salt with their chips	"You always take chips with your salt"

Non-literal use of words

Literal use of language gives words their proper meanings. It maintains a consistent meaning regardless of the context.

Non-literal language uses words in a way that deviates from their originally accepted definition to communicate a more complicated meaning. Essentially, the non-literal use of words is processed in the brain the exact same way as humour is.

Non-literal statement	Actual meaning
He runs like a bullet	He runs very fast compared to most others
Hold your horses	Be patient
You got out of the wrong side of bed	It appears you are having a bad day
You are on pins and needles	You appear anxious and nervous
You crack me up	You make me laugh

The brain will try and visualise the movement and context needed to create a mental representation to understand the sarcastic or non-literal statement. As the atypically myelinated motor and mirror neurons may take longer than the 0.2 seconds to generate the visualisation needed to understand the statement, the brain will then go to the memories part of the brain to try and understand the statement better. For example, *"Hold your horses"* may mean some autistic people start to think about the last time they held a horse, asking themselves *"When did I ever hold a horse? Why would someone hold horses, that would be dangerous to hold horses, and why even think I would hold horses?"* The opportunity to figure out the statement has well surpassed the 0.2 second time period which may trigger frustration and anxiety.

References

1. Torres, E. and Whyatt, C., 2018. Autism: The movement-sensing perspective. 1st ed. Boca Raton : CRC Press, Taylor & Francis Group, (2018).
2. Panksepp, Jaak. "Chapter 11." Affective Neuroscience: The Foundations of Human and Animal Emotions, Oxford University Press, Oxford Et Al., 2014.
3. Https://Www.frontiersin.org/Articles/10.3389/Fpsyg.2013.00296/Full#:~:Text=Notably%2C%20imagination%20not%20only%20has,via%20a%20%E2%80%9Csimulation%E2%80%9D%20process.
4. Stevenson, R.A., Toulmin, J.K., Youm, A. et al. Increases in the autistic trait of attention to detail are associated with decreased multisensory temporal adaptation. Sci Rep 7, 14354 (2017). https://doi.org/10.1038/s41598-017-14632-1
5. Gibson, J. J. (1979). The ecological approach to visual perception. Boston: Houghton Mifflin.
6. Maranesi M, Bonini L and Fogassi L (2014) Cortical processing of object affordances for self and others' action. Front. Psychol. 5:538. doi: 10.3389/fpsyg.2014.00538https://www.frontiersin.org/articles/10.3389/fpsyg.2014.00538/full#h6
7. Panksepp, Jaak. "Chapter 11." Affective Neuroscience: The Foundations of Human and Animal Emotions, Oxford University Press, Oxford Et Al., 2014.
8. Libet B. How does conscious experience arise? The neural time factor. Brain Res Bull. 1999 Nov-Dec;50(5-6):339-40. doi: 10.1016/s0361-9230(99)00143-4. PMID: 10643426.

9. Swanson, L. W. (2003). Brain architecture: Understanding the basic plan. Oxford University Press.

10. Panksepp, Jaak, et al. "Chapter 6." The Archaeology of Mind: Neuroevolutionary Origins of Human Emotions, W. W Norton, New York, 2012.

11. Peterson, Jordan B. "Chapter 2." Maps of Meaning, Taylor and Francis, S.I., 2002.

12. "Chapter 2." Maps of Meaning, Taylor and Francis, S.I., 2002, p. 67.

13. Rizzolatti G, Luppino G. The cortical motor system. Neuron. 2001 Sep 27;31(6):889-901. doi: 10.1016/s0896-6273(01)00423-8. PMID: 11580891.

14. "Https://Www.sciencedirect.com/Science/Article/Abs/Pii/ S1053811907005265?via%3Dihub."

15. Gerardin, E. "Partially Overlapping Neural Networks for Real and Imagined Hand Movements." Cerebral Cortex, vol. 10, no. 11, 2000, pp. 1093–1104., https://doi.org/10.1093/cercor/10.11.1093.

16. https://www.jordanbpeterson.com/docs/230/2014/17Gray.pdf

Chapter 13
The two hemispheres of the brain

This chapter explains the difference of attention styles between autistic and neurotypical people. This chapter has been heavily influenced by the work of Iain McGilchrist, and I would direct people to his book *The Master and his Emissary* for a deeper understanding of the brains two hemispheres [1].

Although the two hemispheres have many similarities, they also have subtle but fundamental differences that help the overall functioning of the brain. The right hemisphere helps the brain perceive the wider context and associated meaning. For example, it sees the whole but not all the individual parts that make it so. The left hemisphere helps the brain focus on specific isolated things, only focusing attention on one thing at a time. For example, it doesn't see the organised whole, it only perceives the individual parts. An analogy that might help understand the difference between the two hemispheres is the right is like a widespread flashlight enabling perception to see the wider context. The left is more like a narrow laser beam enabling perception to be fixed on one isolated thing.

Figure 21: The two hemispheres of the brain

The left is hemisphere is more dominant with order; the things already known.

- Narrowed, laser beam attention
- Breaks things into parts
- Dislikes change, prefers order
- Facts

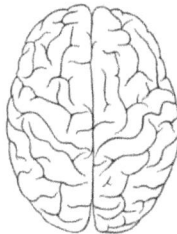

The right hemisphere is more dominant creativity (chaos): anything new and different.

- Sees the wider context
- Sees the relationship of things
- Can deal with change
- Uses imagination and intuition to help decide what to do

The two hemispheres work together to help the person develop the right levels of attention needed for different tasks. For example, sometimes it is best to try and understand the wider context of something, other times it may be necessary to be extremely focused on only one thing, and at times the two need to work closely together. Perception and attention processes starts with the right hemisphere, then left and then back to the right (R-L-R) [1].

It is the right hemisphere that initially detects the whole (the gestalt) and the wider context of what is initially perceived. Then, the left hemisphere uses its narrowed attention span to focus and identify the individual parts of the whole, and this is then communicated to the right hemisphere, helping the right develop a richer understanding of what was originally perceived. For example, the two hemispheres work together to support communication The right hemisphere generates the overall thought about what to say. This is then supported by the left hemisphere as the left collects the isolated words that helps the right assemble a sentence that ensures what the person says is coherent and sensical. The interconnection between the two hemispheres helps the overall brain understand the wider context and individual parts needed for communication. It appears that general perception and attention for anything follows R-L-R processes [1].

The corpus callosum is what connects the two hemispheres together. It is made up of 200 million myelinated neurons, helping the two hemispheres communicate (R-L-R). It does this by inhibiting one hemisphere for the other to take the lead role [1]. Research is continuing to demonstrate atypical myelination patterns of the corpus callosum within autistic brains, which in part may explain the difficulty for the autistic brain to engage in R-L-R processing.

In his book *The Master and his Emissary*, Ian McGilchrist explains if there is any difficulty in right hemisphere functioning, then that person will experience difficulty understanding the context and the associated relationships of things which will result in difficulty with executive functioning skills when dealing with change, anything new or unknown [1].

During the first two years of life the right hemisphere is more myelinated compared to the left. The extra myelination supports explorative motor movement and is therefore closely linked with the development of embodied cognition and social play [1]. The explorative behaviour helps develop awareness of how the body interacts with things, objects and people in the environment, and this function is mainly located in the right hemisphere. This can explain why the right hemisphere eventually becomes specialised to help the brain perceive the wider context, associations and relationships of things to the whole. This is because explorative behaviour is exploring the wider context, exploring possibilities, exploring anomalies, exploring new ways of doing things and even mentally exploring new ideas. It is also during this stage of development (0-2 years) that researchers are continuing to highlight that poor explorative behaviour in babies will likely result in a future autism diagnosis [2]. This highlights a possible corelation between myelination periods and autism.

Autism B Theory claims atypically myelinated motor neurons during the sensory motor stage of development (0-2 years) will mean lifelong difficulty for the autistic brain to engage the right hemisphere (within 0.2 seconds) that support overall brain functioning (R-L-R). Instead, what often happens within the autistic brain is the left hemisphere will become more dominant, particularly in times of stress, change and confusion. This will mean that autistic people will at times struggle to see the whole context, the relationship between things and the overall meaning. Below are some examples of the difference between the two hemisphere functions.

Left hemisphere	Right hemisphere
Left attention sees things in isolation.	Right attention sees the wider context and relationship to things.
Only sees the parts of the body.	Sees the body as a whole.
Prefers things in a static mechanical way. Likes to build the whole through sequencing individual parts.	Emotional understanding of self and others. Embodied sense of emotion. Develops and supports imitation.
Identifies component parts without wider context.	Understands facial expressions, gestures, pitch, tone and body language.

Understands the explicit meaning of words.	Understands the implicit meaning of what is said. Helps mental imagery of self and others to problem solve, imagine and think (Executive function skills). Visual information helps the right see the wider context and relation to things.
When it is only the left hemisphere that is activated it can be difficult to recognise people should they have changed their appearance (different haircut, style, fashion, beard). The left hemisphere has difficult joining all the individual parts to a whole.	Sees the context and relationship of individual parts which means if small changes happen to isolated parts, the right hemisphere can still see the whole. This helps the brain recognise people who may have changed their appearance.
Wants to break time into pieces and sequences.	Perceives time in a flow state, something that is lived.
Sees things in static states. Can experience palinopsia: the repeated reoccurrence of a visual image after it has been seen. It is also like seeing a flowing image in sequenced static parts. Sometimes it is referred to as visual snow.	Sees things in flow. Helps visuospatial processing. Helps perceive time and spaces, helps mentally generate a 3D map and understanding of things. Helps process things in the future, helps create mental distance of thoughts and upcoming events.
Doesn't think. Even if it isn't the best approach it will fill the gaps of knowledge with things it already has experienced to deal with problems.	Higher degree of wider neural connections which helps make connections to wider context.
More closer local neural connections, helps with closed attention span.	Processes humour, sarcasm and non-literal word use. Processes theory of mind and empathy.

Autistic people will be able to use both hemispheres to help develop overall context, but during times of stress, sensory sensitivity or too many demands the autistic brain will start to become more left hemisphere dominant.

As discussed in previous chapters, atypical myelination patterns may trigger the old brain mechanisms for safety. As already explained, if the brain can't decide what to do, especially when faced with something new, the old brain will start the process of anxiety, gradually increasing negative feelings as each 0.2 seconds pass. Therefore, the brain starts to access the left hemisphere to try and help decide what to do. This is because the left hemispheres narrowed attention will only focus on things it knows, therefore resulting in the person reverting back to doing things it knows as safe. So, when an autistic person is faced with a challenge they don't know how to overcome, instead of the brain hemisphere processing being R-L-R to support executive function skills, the autistic brain will eventually become more left hemisphere dominant for that issue at hand. At times this can be helpful, however, without support from the right hemisphere the left will always believe it is correct. This is because the left hemisphere can't see or understand the wider context. This can explain why some autistic people can often act in a way that seems out of context to the situation.

If the autistic person's thinking is left hemisphere dominant for a period of time, they will experience significant distress if they have to change their focus during this time regardless of how big or small the change is. This can help explain why there are times when some autistic people can tolerate changes but struggle other times. If there are no competing demands the autistic brain might be able to engage in R-L-R processing, helping the autistic person understand the wider context and therefore be able to understand change better.

Any difficulty with R-L-R processing will make generalising very difficult. To generalise people need to make connections between things. This involves seeing and understanding the wider context and the potential relationships of things, skills, activities and people as this helps people transfer skills and experiences from one setting into another. Some autistic people may only associate a certain skill or activity happening in one setting, for example:

- An autistic child may have started travelling to school in a red car. The parents then get a new blue car, but now the autistic person refuses to go to school. It could be the autistic person hasn't been able to generalise that any car can transport them to school, not just a red car.
- An autistic child may have been taught to wash themselves with a green bar of soap, and when the parents change soap (now white), the child may refuse to wash. It could be they have not generalised that soap can be different colours.
- An autistic person may only eat certain foods on certain days. For example, they only ever eat fish fingers on a Thursday and pizza on a Friday. They have not generalised that food doesn't have to be eaten on certain days, instead they can be eaten on various days.
- An autistic person may keep buying the same shoes and becomes

distressed that those shoes are no longer available. The autistic person may have failed to make the generalisation that it is okay to purchase other types of shoes.

This is why it is essential to get the balance right between literal and non-literal use of language. When words such as always, exactly, every, never and none are used, they effectively limit the potential for autistic people to generalise from the absolute context they were originally used in. For example, "*never say no to a teacher*", may mean an autistic people may never be able to say no to any teacher. This is why words such as likely, may, often, sometimes, possibly and various others can really help autistic people understand things can be predictable but not absolute which helps them understand context better.

Dominant left hemisphere processing can explain behaviours such as punding [1]. This is when people engage in repetitive and mechanical assembling and disassembling of inanimate objects such as torches, plugs, figures, computers, machines and various others. It can also manifest itself in people lining up symmetrical structures of objects, for example toys, toy cars, boxes and various others. Both behaviours are highly prevalent within autism.

Dominant left hemisphere processing may also result in difficulties with social interactions. For example, difficulties processing all the facial parts of another person's face may result in temporary prosopagnosia (facial blindness or only seeing some elements of facial parts at times).

A delay in R-L-R function can explain why some autistic people struggle with communication. The right hemisphere generates the overall thought about what to say. This is then supported by the left hemisphere as the left collects the isolated words that helps the right assemble a sentence that ensures what the person says is coherent and sensical. As verbal dialogue is instantaneous, there needs to be constant R-L-R processing just to maintain a conversation. Therefore, any delay or atypical function of the R-L-R hemisphere process could impact on a person's ability to verbally communicate, or even communicate at all. Some people may not be able to talk, some may be only able to talk sometimes, and others may not be able to communicate verbally but can communicate effectively with Augmented and Alternative Communication supports (AAC). Augmented communication support adds to someone's speech, for example, gestures, sign language, facial expressions and body language. Alternative communication support replaces someone's speech, for example pointing boards, Picture Exchange Communication System PECS, communication books, text, computer generated speaking devices and apps, symbol communication systems and eye gaze technology.

Figure 22 demonstrates the general difference between R-L-R attention, and left hemisphere dominant attention.

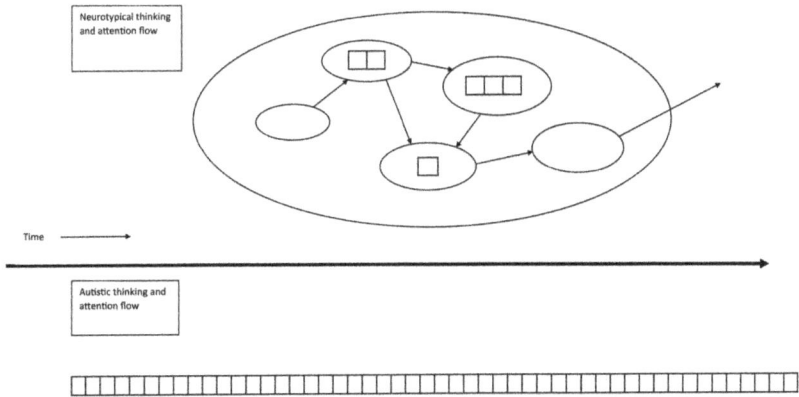

Generally, R-L-R is the natural attention style. This helps the person see the wider context, how things are connected, that things can overlap and change but they still flow. This helps understand the relationship of many things at any one time. This can be helpful when flexibility and change is needed, however, there may be times when attention needs to be narrowed to focus on isolated parts. Alternatively, if autistic people have experienced too much stress, are overloaded, or haven't had the chance to stim or regulate, their brain will then default to left hemisphere attention thinking only. This will often mean the autistic brain will see things in isolation, breaking up the whole into small linear parts to work through. Such an approach can be useful for things that require significant detailed attention but it often prevents the autistic person from seeing the context (the bubble) in which other things are nested in. There are many benefits to such incredible attention, but it is often time consuming, energy draining and impacts on understanding of relationship context and time.

Left hemisphere thinking can explain why some autistic people may only see parts of faces but not see the face as a whole, or only focus on one element of social communication at any one time. It can help explain why people may like to dissemble things and rebuild, it can help explain the amazing feats of precision and artistry. R-L-R processing supports top-down thinking. L-R-L processing supports bottoms-up thinking. This is because L-R-L processes sees the individual parts and slowly builds the context from the bottom up.

Also, as the left hemisphere is very dominant, it can be very hard to shift its attention to something else. Such focus locks people into a small attention tunnel. This is why introducing change can result in extreme stress for people.

The two hemisphere processes are reflected in mythology and philosophy, the most obvious being themes of Order versus Chaos (Left hemisphere associated with order and the right hemisphere associated with creative chaos). Too much order will mean things become static and therefore people will push for change (creative chaos). However, too many changes often result in chaos and feelings of anxiety. Too much creativity results in things being too unpredictable and as a result people will then want to install some sort of order. When the two hemispheres are working together it helps people have a sense of order and stability that gives them a safe base to explore creative new ideas (chaos), as well as new life experiences that help the person grow and develop [2].

The proximal zone of development

The proximal zone of development is basically when a person has enough structure (order and predictability) in their life while still being able to experience some change (creativity [chaos]) that helps them grow and develop. If things are too orderly then life becomes too predictable and boring. This is why new ideas and concepts have to be introduced to keep people intrigued, interested and curious with life. This is how children grow and learn.

During development, caregivers are always setting mini challenges for children. This is done by setting the complexity of tasks (or games) slightly out of the current ability and comfort zone of the child, stretching their ability each time they engage with the activity. Such an approach is always encouraging the child to learn a bit more compared to the last time. The level of stretching is little but often; just enough to challenge the child without upsetting or causing them anxiety. If the task set is beyond their ability, the child will become very anxious as they do not have the ability to problem solve. The trick is to increase the complexity of tasks each time without triggering anxiety. Such an approach allows children to explore with intrigue as they have a safe base to do so. This helps develop the child's worldview, become solution focused which helps develop resilience with problem-solving ability into later life [3]. Such a process is also how adults optimally learn. For example, if an adult wanted to learn a foreign language at a class, the teacher would initially teach very basic words, gradually increasing the complexity as each lesson continues in a curious and playful way. If the teacher sets the task of learning complex words too quickly, and with strict authority, then the adult learner will likely experience negative emotion and may stop engaging. Regardless of the person's age, ability or IQ, helping the person learn in a fun, curious and playful way is the best approach to help people grow and learn, especially autistic people.

Using the autistic person's interests within teaching and support can give real meaning for the autistic person. This is because you are integrating all the emotional systems during the activity in a positive way. Initial learning of any kind may be overwhelming, but a safe and predictable environment then allows the autistic person to overcome initial anxiety. Through interests the autistic person's curiosity, play and seeking systems will help the person experience positive emotion when engaging with new and novel things. Such approaches help regulate the negative aspects of emotions.

Regulation of all emotions in the right context can give real meaning to life as it is emotions that reveal what is important. This is why humans love the creative arts. Music, theatre, drama, storytelling, poetry, art and creative exploration of nature and the cosmos help humans experience emotions in a deep and meaningful way. This may explain why some autistic people develop strong bonds in relation to special interests, helping them express and articulate their thoughts and feelings in a way much more liberating than words. Such interests can convey a deep emotional connection.

Some autistic brains will push for order and rationalism where it can. This can explain why some autistic people prefer to focus on logic with things such as maths, physics, science, facts, engineering, computing, system-based approaches and various meta narratives such as medicine, psychology and philosophy. All are rational and logical, and this can help promote mental balance and wellbeing. This has resulted in some great scientific breakthroughs by autistic people. For example, the Theory of Relativity (Einstein) the Gravitational Constant (Newton), the Theory of Evolution and Natural Selection (Darwin), Alternating Current Electricity (Telsa), Microsoft products (Bill Gates), Apple products (Steve Jobs), and various others. However, some autistic people may have a tendency for creative expression. This could be through things such as playing an instrument, singing, writing, poetry, painting, drawing or creating things. For example, the Sistine Chapel (Michelangelo), Barcelona Cathedral (Goa), Wolfgang Amadeus Mozart's music, Nintendo's Pokémon (Satoshi Tajiri) are all examples of such creative endeavours by autistic people.

It is important to understand that not every autistic person will have special or savant talents, every autistic person will be different. However, what seems to be the case is autistic people seem to be more inclined to gravitate towards sciences and artistic creativity. The most important thing to remember is that each person, regardless of their ability or IQ, should be supported in a way that is sensitive to their own needs and world view. Regardless of the level of the person's ability, if someone tends to gravitate towards a certain discipline (sciences, creative arts or a specialist interest), then this should be supported with the understanding that such a pursuit by that autistic person gives them real meaning to their life, often beyond the person's verbal articulation.

People often confuse special interests with repetitive behaviours. Initially it can be hard to separate the two, but with careful observation a distinction can be made.

Repetitive behaviours

Some autistic people may watch the same films or TV shows on constant repeat, repeating songs or music albums, opening up all cupboards and doors to see what's inside and insistent on certain routines happening such as travelling the same roads or visiting the same shops on specific days and times. All of these behaviours are often examples of the person trying to create structure in what they perceive as a chaotic world.

Some autistic people may have significant challenges. This could be extreme sensory sensitivities, pain management, emotional regulation, distressed behaviour and challenges with communicating needs (little to no speech and only the use of vocalisations). Having such difficulties will often mean the world is a painful, terrifying and chaotic place.

Such chaotic experiences may result people imposing extreme order in their life. Essentially they are trying to make the world more predictable as this will help reduce anxiety and panic. Often the only way some people autistic can impose order is to reduce their world to a smaller predictable place. For example, they may avoid going to certain places, eventually stop attending school, day support, clubs, stop mixing with other people, only wear the same clothes, only eat the same foods, insist on certain routines being followed, turn day into night and some may hardly ever leave their bedroom. Some people may even block out other people entirely. For profound needs (people with little or unintelligible speech), some people may instill order in their life by engaging in continuous self-stimming repetitive behaviours such as constant walking, tapping, rocking, finger flicking, obsessive play with gadgets with things like toys, strings and switches. Some people may even develop rhythmical breathing patterns. These behaviours are often the only thing that some people have control over, and therefore becomes a major part of their daily life.

This is why appropriate support is essential for autistic people. Without the right levels of support autistic people could fall into a chaotic state which will result in them forcing order in their life. This may initially help avoid anxiety in the short term, but as time progresses it will make any change even more difficult.

Perceived IQ

There are autistic people with high, average and low IQ levels. There are different estimations about what is the ratio is of autistic people and IQ, however, viewing autistic people through a lens of IQ often reduces families and professionals from thinking about what may be potentially possible for that person.

There are plenty of examples of autistic people who were previously assumed to have had a lower-than-average IQ but with sensitive and caring support have gone onto demonstrate above average IQ levels. For example, some people have attained degrees of education, creative endeavours and employment. Others may not talk but can code computer programmes. Others may have difficulty with literacy skills but have excellent verbal articulation of facts and details around specific interests. Some people may have difficulty with reading but can play many instruments without any tuition. Others may have difficulty with social situations but can write the most beautiful stories and poems. This is why autism should not be viewed through a prism of IQ.

References

1. McGilchrist, Iain. The Master and His Emissary: The Divided Brain and the Making of the Western World. Yale University Press, 2019.
2. Torres, E. and Whyatt, C., 2018. Autism: The movement-sensing perspective. 1st ed. Boca Raton : CRC Press, Taylor & Francis Group, (2018).
3. "Chapter 2." Maps of Meaning, Taylor and Francis, S.I., 2002.

Chapter 14
Autism and mental health

Around 80% of autistic people will experience mental health issues at some point during their life [1].

Being different can have advantages, but it can also mean being ridiculed and embarrassed by the majority of society. This often leads to things such as bullying, being taken advantage of, not understood and not fully accepted into society. This can help explain why autistic people are more prone to experiencing trauma and poor mental health.

The exact cause of most mental health issues is too complex to establish in this book, but research suggests that a combination of factors including heredity, biology, psychological trauma and environmental stresses are all likely to be involved in some mental health issues.

The book *The Myth of Mental Illness*, by psychiatrist Thomas Szasz [2], has been credited for highlighting that a significant proportion of poor mental health is from the inability to cope with the demands of daily living rather than being a result of a mental illness or disease.

Mark Solms is a South African psychoanalyst and neuropsychologist. Solms highlights an approach called *One size fits all* as a way to understand the root cause of poor mental health for each individual. This approach is highlighted in Figure 23 [3,4]. This approach highlights that there will be something the person cannot deal with, explaining this will likely be the root cause of their mental health issue. Solms explains there may be more than one problem the person cannot deal with, but his approach can help identify what each of these are.

Figure 23: One size fits all model for understanding poor mental health (Mark Solms)

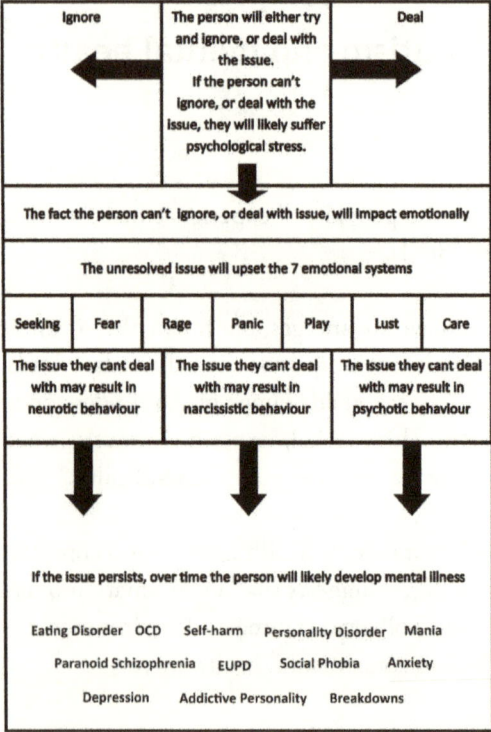

Ignore	The person will either try and ignore, or deal with the issue. If the person can't ignore, or deal with the issue, they will likely suffer psychological stress.	Deal

The fact the person can't ignore, or deal with issue, will impact emotionally

The unresolved issue will upset the 7 emotional systems

Seeking	Fear	Rage	Panic	Play	Lust	Care

The issue they cant deal with may result in neurotic behaviour	The issue they cant deal with may result in narcissistic behaviour	The issue they cant deal with may result in psychotic behaviour

If the issue persists, over time the person will likely develop mental illness

Eating Disorder   OCD   Self-harm   Personality Disorder   Mania

Paranoid Schizophrenia   EUPD   Social Phobia   Anxiety

Depression   Addictive Personality   Breakdowns

For example, if someone is experiencing a problem their first reaction is to see if they can ignore it. If the problem can be ignored then the person does not experience any negative emotion. An example of this is fear of flying … the person avoids flying and therefore doesn't have to deal with the issue.

However, if the issue can't be ignored the person is then forced to deal with it, meaning the person will need to learn something new to deal with the issue. For example, say the person had to fly somewhere for life saving surgery, they are then forced to deal with the issue of flying. An example of dealing with the issue could be the person going to hypnotherapy or CBT therapy to try and overcome the fear of flying. Once the person has learned to deal with the issue they no longer experience negative emotion.

If the person cannot ignore and cannot deal with the issue (they really need to fly and the therapy didn't work), then they will likely suffer poor mental health and psychological distress. If this continues over a prolonged period of time then a mental illness could be likely.

Often the challenges that autistic people can't ignore and can't deal with are related to everyday challenges that most neurotypical people take for granted. For example:

- Sensory overload environments (school, college, work, shops and social gatherings).
- Changes to physical environments (impacting on spatial awareness and sense of body position).
- Communicating choice, wishes and needs.
- Understanding the emotional intention of others.
- Understanding social norms of social interactions, and a fear of getting them wrong.
- Dealing with change, upset of routines and structure.
- Difficulties in planning ahead and time management.
- Difficulties with on-the-spot problem-solving.
- Trying to cope with burnout.

Even things such as playtime, school, college, work placements, lunch breaks, food, house tasks, family get-togethers, going to the shop, relationships, dealing with mail, money and countless other life tasks can all make daily life difficult. Without support some autistic people don't have the option to ignore, or the ability to deal with such aspects of daily living, therefore making autistic people more vulnerable to poor mental health as explained by Figure 23.

Autistic people usually have to develop workaround strategies to cope, and some may have to have rest days throughout the week to prevent burnout. Over time, stress with aspects of daily living will result in a reduction in positive emotions such as the seeking, play and care systems. Eventually the stress will increase the fear, panic and rage systems which will result in the fight, flight and freeze responses being continually activated which will contribute to things such as situational mutism and catatonia.

The model in Figure 24 visually explains how daily challenges can result in poor mental health for autistic people. The model highlights if autistic people are not supported with daily life they will fall into one or more of the three categories:

1. **Crisis (chaos).** The person will frantically try and resolve their difficulties and will often fall into continued crisis's, eventually leading to exhaustion, fatigue and breakdown.
2. **Insistence on strict routines (too much order).** The person will start implementing extreme routines to have some sort of control in their life. Some people will reduce their world more and more to try and make things predictable. This could mean only travelling the same routes, eating the same foods, wearing the same clothes, only using the same rooms and possibly turning night into day to avoid interacting with people. Such behaviours will initially make the person feel better, but such actions mean they haven't learned how to deal with stress and will therefore likely experience continued difficulties in the future.
3. **Crisis cycle.** The person will go between high intense chaotic states of trying to resolve their issues, experience burnout and then resort to installing extreme order to help cope with the burnout. Once the person feels better, this cycle will continue with breakdown highly likely.

When autistic people approach mental health services for support, professionals will usually focus solely on the presenting mental health issue without considering autistic needs around daily living. Mental health professionals often try and treat the autistic person with the evidence-based approaches for that presenting mental health issue (anxiety, depression, OCD and others). The evidenced-based practices are usually based on neurotypical people and are therefore not always applicable for autistic people. This can cause a lot of inner conflict, followed by experiences of hopelessness and loneliness because nobody can help alleviate their poor mental health. For example, treatment for social anxiety encourages the patient to socialise more to practice newly learned social skills. Such an approach does not consider the atypical social development and possible associated difficulties autistic people may have with social situations.

Figure 24: Understanding autism and mental health.

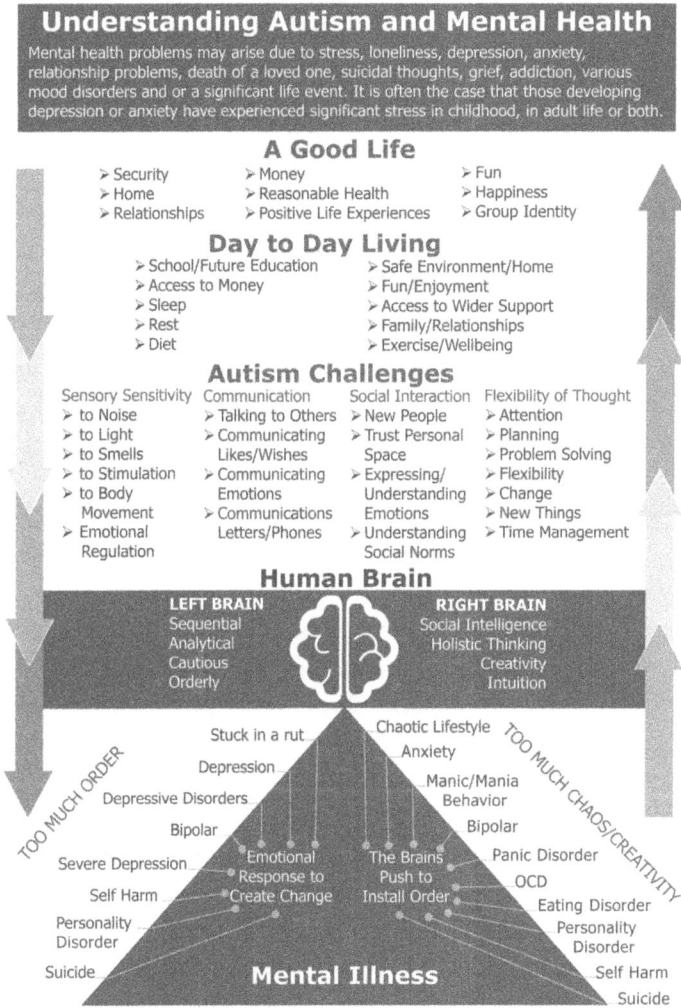

Understanding Autism and Mental Health

Mental health problems may arise due to stress, loneliness, depression, anxiety, relationship problems, death of a loved one, suicidal thoughts, grief, addiction, various mood disorders and or a significant life event. It is often the case that those developing depression or anxiety have experienced significant stress in childhood, in adult life or both.

A Good Life

- Security
- Home
- Relationships
- Money
- Reasonable Health
- Positive Life Experiences
- Fun
- Happiness
- Group Identity

Day to Day Living

- School/Future Education
- Access to Money
- Sleep
- Rest
- Diet
- Safe Environment/Home
- Fun/Enjoyment
- Access to Wider Support
- Family/Relationships
- Exercise/Wellbeing

Autism Challenges

Sensory Sensitivity	Communication	Social Interaction	Flexibility of Thought
to Noise	Talking to Others	New People	Attention
to Light	Communicating Likes/Wishes	Trust Personal Space	Planning
to Smells	Communicating Emotions	Expressing/ Understanding Emotions	Problem Solving
to Stimulation	Communications Letters/Phones	Understanding Social Norms	Flexibility
to Body Movement			Change
Emotional Regulation			New Things
			Time Management

Human Brain

LEFT BRAIN	RIGHT BRAIN
Sequential	Social Intelligence
Analytical	Holistic Thinking
Cautious	Creativity
Orderly	Intuition

TOO MUCH ORDER

Stuck in a rut
Depression
Depressive Disorders
Bipolar
Severe Depression
Self Harm
Personality Disorder
Suicide

Chaotic Lifestyle
Anxiety
Manic/Mania Behavior
Bipolar
Panic Disorder
OCD
Eating Disorder
Personality Disorder
Self Harm
Suicide

TOO MUCH CHAOS/CREATIVITY

Emotional Response to Create Change

The Brains Push to Install Order

Mental Illness

Another example could be the use of Cognitive Behavioural Therapy (CBT). In this therapy CBT uses language such as bad thinking, hot topics, illogical thinking and so forth. Autistic people often struggle with the abstracted ideas based in such language; autistic people often take what is said literally. CBT therapy often results in some autistic people continually self-doubting themselves. For example, the autistic person may wish to stay in the bath for an extra five minutes before doing some housework. As a result of CBT therapy, the autistic person may self-ruminate if wanting to stay in the bath is a bad thought or not. The autistic person may think housework is meant to be important, and if they are enjoying a bath before housework then this could technically be a bad thought. Such self-rumination often results in mental exhaustion and fatigue. CBT can be useful, but any CBT approach should be adapted by a professional who has a good understanding of autism.

The reason why mental health support often fails is because mental health professionals do not consider the source of the presenting mental health issue may be a result of the difficulties autistic people face during daily life. Mental health professionals need to consider and account for the holistic needs of autistic people for mental health therapies to be effective. Such holistic needs should cover:

- Sensory sensitivities.
- Communication preferences, supports and strengths.
- Social interaction preferences, supports and strengths.
- Executive functioning preferences, supports and strengths.
- Attention styles, supports and strengths.
- Supports with daily life tasks (dealing with people, school, college, work, mail, money, utility bills, appointments, authority figures).
- Trauma informed supports.
- Wellbeing (diet, nutrition, health and spirituality).
- Person-centred focus. For example, what does the person wish to achieve; exploring what is meaningful for them.

An often-overlooked form of therapy is autistic lived experience groups. Lived experience from people with similar life events can be really supportive in helping autistic people understand themselves better. This affords the opportunity to learn new ways of successfully coping.

Lived experience groups are excellent ways of empowering autistic people when they are trying to balance the internal conflict of wanting to be independent whilst coming to the realisation they may need support. Having autistic role models talk about their experiences, explaining how they have managed to overcome the difficulties of daily life can help autistic people start to address the source of their poor mental health. Such lived experiences groups are cheap and effective compared to clinical and pharmaceutical interventions.

Support for autistic people is highlighted in appendices 1 and 2.

References

1. https://www.autistica.org.uk/downloads/files/Mental-health-autism-E-LEAFLET.pdf
2. Szasz, Thomas S. The Myth of Mental Illness. PALADIN, 1992.
3. https://iaap.org/wp-content/uploads/2020/01/Mark-Solms-scientific-standing-of-Psa.pdf
4. Solms, Mark. "'Does One Size Fit All? by Prof Mark Solms, Part 1 – Youtube." Does One Size Fit All? by Prof Mark Solms, 29 June 2018, https://www.youtube.com/watch?v=ysQ_yeZMhh0.

Chapter 15
Autism and trauma

What is trauma?

Trauma is an emotional response to an event. There are three main types of trauma: acute, chronic and complex. Acute trauma can happen from a single incident or event. Chronic trauma is repeated incidents or events. Complex trauma is exposure to varied and multiple traumatic events, often of an invasive and interpersonal nature.

Autism and trauma

Autistic people will likely have some degree of difficulties with sensory sensitivities, communication, social interactions, and flexibility of thought, especially within a neurotypical environment. There will be things autistic people are forced to deal with on a daily basis which may be difficult. The complexity of daily life is enough to make autistic people more vulnerable to trauma compared to others. Below are some examples of how autistic people may be more vulnerable to trauma.

Sensory sensitivities

Attending school, shops or places of work may be an overwhelming experience resulting in sensory overload. Such overload on a daily basis could result in chronic trauma.

Communication

Experiences of communicating with authorities (social services, schools, head teachers, police, lawyers) can be traumatic. An example could be when an autistic person was trying to communicate honestly but eventually found themselves in some sort of conflict which created traumatic memories relating to people of authority and power. Such traumatic experiences are enough to make the person so self-conscious it stops them from asking for help which may create vulnerabilities in the future.

Social Interactions

Previous experiences of difficult social interactions could be from the playground, school, clubs, supermarkets, family get togethers, lunch breaks at work, relationship breakdowns and various others. Previous difficult experiences may result in the person constantly worrying about what to say and how to act in future social situations. This can be so overwhelming that the person may start to experience ongoing chronic complex trauma which will likely result in the person avoiding social interactions in the future.

Flexibility of thought (executive function skill)

Experiences of not being able to problem-solve or plan ahead can often cause traumatic experiences. An example could be going for a medical procedure. Say the experience was distressing because the medical practitioner did not fully inform the person about what was to happen (needles, flashes, touching and undressing). This could result in a traumatic invasive experience (acute trauma). This may result in the next medical appointment being fraught with stress and anxiety.

Longer term effects of trauma can include difficulty with emotional regulation, flashbacks, blocked memory recall, strained relationships, disembodiment, fractured perception, burnout, headaches and nausea [1].

People who are exposed to ongoing trauma will continually have their fight, flight and freeze responses activated. Danger doesn't need to be present to activate stress and anxiety. Danger can also be remembered or imagined [2]. The constant anxiety of remembering traumatic events, or anticipating how to overcome similar future events will continually result in anxiety and panic.

Traumatic experiences may be enough to put the body in constant fight, flight or freeze responses. For example, people may experience the following:

- Fight. The person may be aggressive, challenging, irritable, argumentative and short tempered.
- Flight. They may run away and engage in avoidance behaviour.
- Freeze. The person may experience immobilisation of body parts, also known as a catatonic state. Variations of the freeze response can be selective and situational mutism, pseudo-seizures, brain fog and non-engagement.

Such experiences disables the person from perceiving social signs of safety such as smiling faces, warm tone of voice and positive body language. This will further impact on the person's ability to safely engage with others.

It is useful to assume that most autistic people may have experienced trauma in their background. It is best to use an informed trauma approach when supporting autistic people. Being trauma informed is:

- Being a safe person and building trust. Do what you say you will and mean what you say. This helps build confidence, trust, and cooperation.
- Smiling. It displays positive signs of emotion.
- Avoiding harsh judgements and negative body language. Instead, use soft trusting words. For example, avoid statements such as *"That's rubbish... how stupid ... shouldn't have done that"*, instead you could say things like *"That sounds as if it was difficult... what did you learn from that... what would you do differently?"*

Being a safe person, building trust, smiling and displaying positive signs of emotions such as open body language and a friendly demeanour will help switch off the fight, flight and freeze responses experienced by the person. Being a safe person will mean you are helping the person have a much better chance of connecting which will help activate the signs of safety in the person's brain which will help them overcome their traumatic experiences better.

References

1. A., Van der Kolk Bessel. The Body Keeps the Score: Brain, Mind, and Body in the Healing of Trauma. Penguin Books, 2015.
2. Levine, Peter A. Healing Trauma: A Pioneering Program for Restoring the Wisdom of Your Body. ReadHowYouWant, 2012.

Conclusion

Autism B Theory explains all the diversity seen within the autistic spectrum while still being flexible enough to help people understand autism in relation to each autistic person.

It is hoped that the theory can help focus research to develop the most appropriate supports for autistic people.

Researchers have often tried to establish a biological marker for autism. This worries autistic people because such an approach inevitable leads to talk of eugenic cleansing. Hopefully Autism B Theory can finally close the debate around eugenics by explaining that autism is a naturally occurring phenomena resulting from the biological demands of pregnancy. It could even be argued that the biological demands is nature's way of ensuring neurodiversity. Humanity has benefited greatly from neurodiversity, therefore an appreciation of all neurodiversity can only help all of humanity ... this is what the book has tried to achieve.

Hopefully the ideas and suggestions in this book can inspire current and future research to start focusing on what will help autistic people the most. With the right support autistic people can begin to enjoy a life that is enjoyable and meaningful for them.

Support strategies for autistic people are explained in appendix one, and strategies for neurotypical people to support autistic people are explained in appendix two.

Appendix 1
Autistic self-supports

This appendix highlights support strategies for autistic people. Not every strategy will help or make sense to you, but there may be ones that do. Just use the ones that help the most.

Thinking about going for an autism diagnosis

You've probably always felt a bit different compared to others, that somehow you didn't fit in, that your ideas, thoughts, passions and interests were different to others. This is often when people start to think they might be autistic.

Thinking about going for a diagnosis can be intimidating. For example, you may ask yourself, "What will change? How will people treat me? Will friends and family treat me differently? What support might be available? What does the process involve?"

Often people explain the sense of relief when diagnosed as it helps them understand their life experiences better. For some it is also relieving to know that there is nothing wrong with them, they are only autistic.

Disclosing you are autistic

Some people initially find it difficult telling other people they are autistic, yet others explain it can be a relief. If you do disclose you are autistic you may have people ask you questions about it. If you are comfortable answering questions about being autistic then it is your decision to do so. You are also entitled not to tell people that you are autistic if that is your preference.

Many autistic people have explained they have had to hide their autistic identity due to the worry of being ridiculed or excluded. Often autistic people, even people yet to be diagnosed, try and act normal to fit in. Autistic people explain it is as if they are projecting a false persona, masking and acting in a way that they feel other people expect of them. Autistic people explain that this type of masking can develop from a very early age. However, masking can come at a cost. For example, some autistic people have explained that they have had to develop interests in things they don't like just so they can fit in.

Some autistic people will copy and mimic what others are doing, telling themselves *"If they are doing that then I must do the same"* This can cause confusion because the person is acting in a way that feels alien to them. Some people have masked for so long that they now struggle to make sense of their true identity. Over time this can lead to burnout and poor mental health. For example, people may have tolerated sensory overload, or put themselves in unsafe situations with things like bad relationships or drug and alcohol dependency to try and fit in.

Some autistic people believe others should openly identify as being autistic as this will prevent or significantly reduce the need to mask. Other autistic people explain they feel it is safer to mask as it can reduce stigma and ridicule. Some people mask sometimes, and just be their autistic self in other times. You have to do what is right for you.

To help make the decision you may ask yourself, *"Is the benefit of pretending and masking better than just being my natural autistic-self in front of others?"* Only you can answer that question. It may be helpful to discuss such approaches with people you trust. If possible, find out what other autistic people have said (internet search, social media, books). Try and get the views of various people to ensure you have a wider perspective.

Some people feel reassured when they are open about being autistic as they become aware there are many other autistic people just like them. Other people may have difficulty accepting they are autistic. For example, some people have been diagnosed before they were ready to fully accept such affirming news. Some people may need time to adjust, but eventually people often say they wish they knew they were autistic sooner.

Some people can experience a sense of loss and mourning once diagnosed. This is because the person looks back over their lives and often feel sadness for their younger self, remembering the painful lessons when trying to fit in. Painful and traumatic memories are often associated with bullying at school, abuse, relationship breakdown, missed employment and other life opportunities. Care and understanding needs to be given to newly diagnosed people to ensure they are emotionally supported.

Disclosing you are autistic is your own personal choice, that is why there is no specific guidance on who you should disclose to. You may get different responses from different people when you disclose you are autistic. For example, *"Ah, that's cool, I have an autistic family member... Sorry, you don't look autistic... I would never have known... Isn't autism just a myth... No way you could have autism".*

Often, any ingenuine comments are usually coming from naivety as it is unlikely the person is deliberately trying to upset you. This is why some people find it useful to rehearse a pre-set description about autism. For example, autistic people use different phrases to describe their autistic disposition such as autistic, auty, aspie, on the spectrum, neurodivergent and various others. The best advice is to use whatever phraseology makes sense to you, and explain what autism means to you if you want to talk about autism. Be prepared for some questions, but remember, you are entitled to tell people that you do not want to discuss autism if you don't want to.

If you do decide to tell some people you are autistic, remember that you don't need to tell every aspect of your autistic experience, only tell people what you think applies to that particular situation or relationship. For example, extra supports at school or work could help so it may be helpful to disclose you are autistic to a teacher or employer. Also, telling a healthcare professional may help them make adjustments which may greatly benefit you. It is easier for professionals and agencies to support you better if they know you are autistic, but it is your decision to decide who to disclose to.

Attention

Autistic people are capable of very focused attention around a singular thing. Such focus and attention help achieve a flow state of productivity. Such flow states of intense attention can often be enjoyable as it feels like an escape from the neurotypical world.

You may have focused attention with certain things. You may have super focus around one or two things at any one time and this may be beneficial for what you're focussing on, but be mindful that this attention may be preventing you from doing other things. Your latest interest, job or hobby may mean you're spending all your time on this and neglecting other areas of your life such as a work-life balance, relationships and overall health. For example, you may be so focused that you are forgetting to eat, sleep or go to the toilet. Therefore, try and make time to be present to yourself and your bodily needs. Try and factor in regular intervals and remind yourself of the wider context of what you are doing or should be attending to. For example, *"this is a job, and I will be back tomorrow to finish"*, or *"this* [hobby] *will still be available after my dinner"*. Focus and attention is good, but balance is needed.

Context. Remember, you may only be able to focus your attention on one or two things at any one time so there may be things you may have missed or forgotten to do. Reminders in diaries, calendars, alarms and display boards can help remind you of the wider context of other important areas of your life.

Guidance for when the rules change

Generally speaking, autistic people struggle with change, including the flexible nature of social interactions.

It is often the unclear, unknown and anything ambiguous that creates anxiety, therefore, having rules provides a rigid structure that makes things predictable. However, what tends to happen is other people often don't follow pre-established rules or they change them without telling you. The uncertainty results in distress and anxiety. People will often change rules to make something better or easier, therefore, instead of trying to remember all the rules, it is best to change your attitude to rules.

Rules help bring structure, but they need updated from time-to-time to enable positive change to happen. It is therefore naive to think of rules as absolutes, it is better to think of them as *guidance for the time being*. Guidance can help bring clarity and structure just like a rule but reduces frustration and anxiety. Also, guidance prevents thinking in black and white terms, instead it allows the opportunity to understand the wider context often missed.

When someone changes a rule or a pre-established way of doing something, instead of becoming angry or upset, remind yourself that it is better to understand the reason for it rather than just reacting negatively to it. Remind yourself that the recent change is to benefit someone or something, and ask yourself, who or what is this change benefitting? This will help you develop a wider understanding of why the change may have happened.

If you can't figure out the need for the rule change you can ask someone. Explain to the person you want to understand the reasons why the change took place. Ask someone to explain it to you in the fullest context possible. Ask them why the change is beneficial and if it could be beneficial for you, and if so, why? Sometimes changes can be beneficial once they're understood. Think of all the opportunities you've missed because you didn't clearly understand them.

You can tell when someone is taking advantage of you or a situation in relation to change. If the changes are explained in the fullest context, then you will be able to understand if the change is of benefit to you or others. If the change does benefit you in some way then at least there is some logical reason for the change. Alternatively, if the person making the change is doing so to benefit themselves and not you, then it is possible they are taking advantage of you. If so, politely and calmly assert the reasons why such changes do not benefit you. The four tips to being assertive are:

- Be specific about what you are communicating.
- Explain why it is important to you and for you.
- Be respectful to the other person, no need to shout.
- Try and act confidently, even if you are nervous.

The rest of the strategies in the following pages will help you deal with change better.

Change

Often autistic people use black and white thinking. For example, *it must be this way.*

Instead of seeing any change as an opportunity, you anticipate change with anxiety. You need to be aware that the automatic default of *it must be this way*, may be reducing positive opportunities for you.

Although it is hard, try and look for any positives when experiencing change. Sometimes change can make things better. It is better to be optimistic rather than negative. For example, what is the alternative, always unhappy and resentful? Sometimes change is needed, otherwise you will reduce your world smaller and smaller, limiting new opportunities. Sometimes you need to understand that change may bring new and exciting things into your awareness.

Focus on one thing of the change that is positive, or that you like. Then keep continuing this process bit by bit, focusing on more positive elements of the change.

When change occurs, ask yourself if this change is for the better? For example, you could ask yourself *"Will this change benefit me now or in the future... will my future self be happy with this change ?"* If the answer is yes, then focus on the positives that the change may bring.

It is better to be kind to yourself when going through change. Don't criticise yourself with harsh self-talk. Talk to yourself in a caring manner ...

plenty of reassurance and positivity is much better than constantly putting yourself down.

Sometimes a stern word with yourself (*"C'mon, get through this!"*) can get you through some very difficult challenges, but don't accept this as the default mode for motivated self-talk all of the time because you will eventually burnout. If you do push yourself to get through challenges try and factor in recovery time.

Look for patterns as this may help you adapt to a change quicker. If something happens once, it is a one-off. Twice, it may just be a coincidence. However, if the same thing happens three times it is usually a pattern that will likely repeat.

If you are struggling to decide what to do in relation to a change, ask yourself *"What is best for me to do now and what would be best for me in the future?"* This will help you make a positive decision knowing your future self will be content with the decisions you make.

Having a back-up plan in place can help deal with unexpected changes. If a sudden change happens, just focus on the back-up plan as this will prevent you from becoming overwhelmed. The back-up plan will help you keep functioning towards a safe conclusion you are comfortable with. The back-up plan could be written down in your bag, pocket or stored on your phone. The back-up plan could even just be a reminder to keep safe, for example *"If you are unsure what to do, this is how to make your way home"*, or how to telephone someone for advice, or go somewhere safe. This way you always have a safe option. A backup plan might be enough to stop a full-blown panic attack.

Understanding social norms

Understanding why people engage in social norms and small talk can help you understand people better.

Social norms and small talk basically make social interactions smoother for most neurotypical people. The purpose of these social norms is not to ask questions literally, instead it is to make people more predictable to each other by determining if they will behave in a certain way.

For example, *"How are you… some weather today"* are usually replied with things like *"I'm not bad, how are you… yes some weather it has been."* The generic reply unconsciously tells the other person they will behave in a certain way and will not be a threat. Hence why these questions are never really asked literally. Here is some guidance to help understand social norms and small talk better.

Some people will greet you with statements such as *"How are you… what's up… how's it going… how are you doing?"* These are meant to be pleasant greetings, not actual genuine questions. Usually, an acceptable reply could be *"I'm okay, thanks for asking, I hope you are well,"* and then try and remember the real reason why you are in that place and focus your attention on that.

If you are unsure if the person meant something literally, just ask the person, "Did *you mean that literally?*".

If you have forgot someone's name, or have difficulty pronouncing it, just say so. Maybe try writing down the name if it helps. If at a meeting you could write the names down on a sheet of paper which reflects where each person is sitting as this will help you remember all the names better.

Being on time demonstrates to other people that you are reliable and responsible. A good guide is to try and arrive about five minutes before meeting someone or when attending an appointment. If you are going to be late let the person know if possible. People are usually understanding if they are told about lateness in advance. Sometimes people may be late for you, it may be annoying but sometimes there are genuine reasons why.

You may get frustrated with conflicting statements some people make. For example, people may say things like, *"We need to go to the shops…we need to get going on that… we should be doing that."* The problem with these kinds of statements is that they suggest things should be happening now, but often the people that say such statements don't actually give a timescale for when those things will be done. Such statements are confusing because words like *go* and *doing* are meant to be in the present, they are doing words that require imminent action and this causes inner conflict for some autistic people as they think they should be going but nobody else is moving to go. If you find yourself confused in such situations, just ask the person to explain when they think such action will be undertaken. Seeking clarity and context will hopefully remove confusion.

If you like drinking alcohol because it makes you more sociable, then try and not drink to the extent that you make a fool of yourself or puts you in a vulnerable position.

Communicating with others

Social anxiety refers to feelings of nervousness and panic when communicating with others. Anxiety may happen before, during or after a social occasion. Even just the thought of a social occasion can be anxiety provoking. Some people will use safety behaviours when experiencing social anxiety, others may use social coping strategies.

Safety behaviours

Safety behaviours are the things you do within a situation to try and prevent your fears from becoming reality. Here are some examples of safety behaviours: using headphones so nobody talks to you, using alcohol or drugs to be more confident, constantly making excuses to get out of social encounters, not contributing to discussions/meetings/class, making excuses to leave early, only talking to specific safe people and so on.

You may feel like these tricks of the trade are helpful. They may help short term, but they don't develop skills and confidence for similar future social situations. Strategies are a little different compared with safety behaviours, this is because strategies build confidence over time.

Social coping strategies

The social support strategies highlighted below are only to be used if you think they will help. If you find this too difficult or not authentic, that's fine, only use what you think may be helpful for you.

How to understand others

It is hard to truly know what other people are thinking when socially interacting. Most people fail to accurately understand another person's perspective. This is often when communication breaks down. There is a way to help avoid confusion around communication, Peterson and Rodgers explain there are three points to follow [1]:

1. **Listen to what is being said.**
2. **Summarise back to the person the overall meaning of what you think they said and meant.** Try and do this within a couple of sentences if possible.
3. After you have summarised what you thought the person was saying, **listen to what the person has to say**. The person will either say *"Yes, you've summarised that well… exactly… yes, that is what I was trying to say* [or something to that affect]". If the person doesn't think you've summarised the meaning of what they said they will likely say *"Not quite, what I meant was this… it's more like this…"* This is good because they have now told you what they were thinking and this means you no longer have to guess.

Have something ready to say

If you are nervous about meeting someone (in person, online or texting) think of three (or more if you wish) predetermined topics you can fall back to if the conversation becomes difficult. These predetermined topics can be about something you like, or what you know the person likes, has recently done or whatever you would like to share with that person yourself.

Ending the conversation

There are different ways to end a conversation. It can be as simple as thanking the person(s) for their time, saying it was good to talk with them (if it was, you don't need to if it wasn't) and then say goodbye. You don't always have to give an explanation or make excuses to leave a conversation. You can simply say that you need to go.

People say, *"see you later... speak later"*, without a predetermined arrangement for later. People say such things as it doesn't commit themself to a time or date in the future; it gives the opportunity to engage with the person when it suits them best which is why they say it. Again, if you are unsure if they mean as specific time and date then ask them for clarity. For example, *"Sorry, remind me, have we got something specifically planned to meet?"* The person will then give you clarity.

General points that may help with relationships

Remember, other people will not automatically know what you are thinking, so it is always best to give some context about the thing you are communicating about. Just a sentence or two to explain the context is enough. For example, *"I think this about... and this is the reason why..."* This will help other people understand you better because they have been informed of the wider context.

Don't assume other people know what you want or like, no one knows unless you tell them, so tell them if it helps.

If you are unsure if the person has understood what you said you could ask the person, *"Did that make sense... did I explain that well... is there anything you would like me to clarify?"*

If you are not being respected by others do not tolerate being victimised, bullied or taken advantage of. Speak with someone you trust if you have any doubts or suspicions about the way you are being treated.

You are entitled to tell people no in relation to any uncomfortable jokes, personal approaches or being touched in a sexual nature.

Making decisions

Some people have difficulty making decisions. For example, how do you ever know if you will make a good or bad decision? Of all the decisions that has ever been made, nobody knew with 100% certainty if the decision would eventually be good. A certain amount of time needs to pass before anyone can state if the decision made was good or bad.

People think there are perfect solutions that guarantees perfect results. Nobody makes perfect decisions. Instead of thinking about the perfect decision, think progression.

It is the lack of clarity which often causes anxiety around decision-making. Making decisions quickly and effectively will help bring organisation into your life. The people that get better at decision making are the ones that decide and move on. It is often indecision that causes anxiety and frustration.

If you do make a wrong decision then at least you can learn from it. There is no learning or progression when you haven't made any decision. Maybe another decision would have worked out better, but it could have also worked out worse, you will never know so it is pointless ruminating about it. The important thing is you can learn from decisions once you've made them.

Decisions lead to action and enough action over time means you can get things done which will help bring organisation into your life. If you think you did make the wrong decision, ask yourself, *"what did I learn from that, are there any positives that I can learn from?"* Focus on the positives and move on. You probably ruminate about previous decisions you've made, all that critical self-talk making you feel ashamed. Be more forgiving to yourself.

Sometimes it can be useful to imagine yourself as the third person when making a decision. For example, *"If someone had the same situation and asked me for advice, what would I say?"*

Breaking things down into smaller parts may help with some decisions. Once broken down, start with the thing that makes the most sense. This will help you move onto the next thing.

Looking for patterns helps. If something happens once, it's just a one off. Twice is usually a coincidence, but three times usually suggests a pattern. Patterns are usually a prediction of a phenomenon that will keep repeating over time, and this can help with making decisions about what to do in the future.

When trying to decide what best to do you could ask yourself, *"Will the future me be happy with the decision I am about to make?"* If not, then change it. Will you be proud of the decision in the future? If not, why not? This will help you make better decisions.

If you are unsure about making important decisions, why not ask someone you trust for advice. It is not a sign of weakness asking for advice.

You could also visualise someone you admire giving you advice. You can imagine whoever you wish. It can be someone who has helped you in the past, someone you admire, a friend, a teacher, a colleague, a famous person you've never met, even someone who is no longer alive. You can ask yourself, *"If [person's name] were here, what would they tell me to say, how would they help me make a choice on what needs done?"*

Does the decision tie in with your aims, goals, and values? If not, is it still a good decision?

Getting started is better than no start.

If you can't start something, pause, and ask yourself, what is so hard about this? Ask how is this difficult and what you need to do to at least start. It isn't the lack of motivation that is stopping you making decisions, it is likely the lack of clarity of how to start.

Organising yourself

There are generally two types of people in relation to self-organisation.

1. People who use to-do lists, diaries, schedules and planners.
2. People who use their memory for organising and planning. These people often say they feel judged or pressured when using planners, diaries and schedules.

You may have difficulty organising yourself, therefore a good question to start with is, what type of person are you, a 1 or a 2?

People who use to-do lists, diaries, schedules and planners enjoy and often need this level of organisation. Having this structure in front of them helps them organise themselves better. For example, reminders of when to pay a bill, attend appointments and so on are all recorded to remind them at a future date.

However, for some people such organisational supports cause a lot of anxiety and pressure. This is because they feel like the organisational supports are constantly judging them. It is as if the organisational aids are saying *"You will fail to do all this stuff"*, which is why some people rely only on memory for planning and organising.

If you can use organisational supports then you should. It is best to understand that organisational supports are meant to be a help, not a judge. The structure and organisation such supports will bring to your life will be worth the effort. For example, you may put letters in a drawer because trying to file the letters properly causes too much anxiety. Initially you may feel okay as the letters are out of sight, but the nagging awareness of the letter causing problems for you in the future plays on your mind which makes you more anxious as time goes by. If you do things like this on a regular basis you will continue to experience high anxiety.

Below are examples of organisational supports. If you are not ready to use the organisational supports then try and use some of the informal strategies highlighted later.

Formal strategies to help organise yourself better

Most people don't create a clear plan for their day and the lack of clarity leads to procrastination. This is because the brain doesn't like ambiguity. Ambiguity means the brain will seek out the easiest thing to do hence the procrastination. That's why scheduling your day is important because it provides clarity and avoids procrastination.

When you schedule important tasks it's much more likely you'll work on them. This is why organisational supports are helpful. Below are some examples of organisational aids that might help you structure your day and time better.

To-do lists. To-do lists are a great way of organising yourself and your day ahead. It helps your brain understand what needs done.

To-do list or wish list? Instead of calling it a to-do list, you could call it a wish list. The idea is to help you create the type of day you could wish for. Remember, focus on the positives, for example, *"I wish x could be done... I wish to have x happen today"* and so on.

Diaries. There is far too much stuff to remember, therefore having a diary keeps you organised. Organised people seem super effective; it's because they use diaries, to-do lists and planners effectively. For example, recording appointments and special events will help you remember and plan for them coming. Even recording smaller practical things can help. For example, recording the best before dates of food in a diary will make sure you don't waste food, reminders to wash and clean on certain days and so on. All of this helps bring organisation into your life. You can use such aids to remind you of anything that you feel would help you the most.

Planners, weekly timetables and calendars. Yearly planners can be quite good to have as an overview of what is coming in the weeks and months ahead. It can help you transition and adjust. This can be useful when combined with a daily diary or weekly timetable. A diary often shows you week-to-week, but a yearly planner lets you see everything. Even schedule cards, to-do lists, step-by-step summary guides and tick-lists can help remind you of what you need to do.

Concertina folders. An excellent resource for keeping all your letters and mail in one central place. You could have one folder for letters and mail, and another folder for important documents such as passports, birth certificates and so on.

Dealing with letters and bills

A good system for organising letters is to open letters and act on them quickly. Some people prefer to have a certain day to go through mail as this means they are then in a prepared state to deal with such tasks. Choose what works for you but don't let mail sit for long periods as it will only increase your anxiety.

Once the letter/mail is opened, decide what needs to be done. If it is something to be done soon, add it to your to-do list, if it can wait then add it to your diary, calendar or planner. Also, add a reminder if you think it will help (maybe a few weeks, or a few days in advance may help you slowly adjust to something coming up). Once the action has been assigned to either a to-do list, diary or calendar, file the letter away in the concertina folder under the relevant header. This way you can retrieve the letter at a future date if needed. Once a year you could organise the concertina folder to ensure everything is organised and in date. You can then relax because you have taken care of your letters and mail. The same process can happen with emails, at least once a week open and decide what needs done by recording it on either the to-do list, diary or calendar, then either delete or save the email.

Budgeting skills

A lot of people stress about money which prevents them from organising themselves. Some people don't have any idea of the monies in and out of their accounts. The main reason for this avoidance is due to a lack of clarity. The lack of clarity causes anxiety so the person avoids looking at budgeting altogether. This is not a good approach as it will often lead to increased anxiety and potential money problems in the future. It is best to understand what monies come in and out of your account.

Develop a budget sheet as this will bring more clarity about your finances. A budget sheet can be used for a week or month. You can do this with pen and paper or with the aid of a computer. Develop a budget sheet like this one below:

Item to be considered	Money in	Money out	
Income All sources of income recorded here. For example, wages, benefits and any other regular income. Any one-off payment can be saved in a separate savings account.			
Fixed bills These are bills that you have to pay every week/month. For example, housing costs, mortgage, insurances, transport (car/bus pass/petrol), bills, groceries, gas/electricity, taxes and various others.			
Flexible items These are items that are needed but maybe not the exact same money is spent every month or week. For example, clothes, personal grooming (haircuts/treatments/dental), house furniture and various others.			
Fun /Special interests These are things that you would like but do not need. These are to be afforded only if all other bills can be paid. For example, nights out, gaming, cinema, special interests, books, toys and various others.			
Totals			**What is left over?**

If you are spending more than is coming in then you need to adjust what you are spending. The idea is to ensure you are spending less than what is coming in, that way you will avoid money problems. Ideally, you would have some money left over and this can be saved which will help fund the fun and special interests that you enjoy.

Be realistic with your budgeting estimations; the more honest you are the better the budget plan will work for you.

If you struggle with budgeting then approach someone you trust and ask for help.

There are lots of free basic budgeting courses online. The quicker you start budgeting the quicker you will have more money and freedom from worry. The template above may look basic, but this is the best approach for you to initially understand your finances better.

Informal strategies to help organise yourself better

Some people may avoid using formal organisational aids (diaries, to-do list, planners) because they will potentially highlight failure should the person not fully complete the actions on them. This is why some people experience formal organisational aids as restrictive, judgemental and anxiety provoking. It is best to try and use organisational aids whenever you can. However, if you still struggle using them then you may benefit from using some of the informal strategies highlighted below.

The things about using to-do lists, diaries and schedules is they keep people on a tight timescale. The problem with setting dates yourself means you know you can (consciously or unconsciously) avoid the activity until the last minute or until it becomes an emergency. This is why some people don't use planners and diaries as they know they will leave it to the last minute anyway. If it was recorded in a diary, the diary entry would only make the person feel bad because they know they were leaving it to the last minute. This is often referred to as Parkinson's law.

Parkinson's law basically means that the full allocation of time afforded for completing a task is always used by the person. For example, if you give someone a week to brush a floor some people will likely take the full week to do so. Alternatively, if they had a deadline of brushing the floor within one minute then it would be done within this time. This is because the more time given to complete a task tells the person's brain that less effort is needed until the deadline, which is why some people leave things to the last minute and rush like mad to get things done. However, the person often wishes they acted earlier as the anxiety and panic of rushing at the last moment is too much. This is why such people need to adopt a strategy to avoid procrastination and last-minute panic. If you are this type of person, don't think you are lazy, selfish or stupid. There are reasons why people are like this and it is much more common than you think. It is related to a phenomenon called reactance theory.

Reactance theory explains why some people may experience a negative reaction when exposed to rules, regulations, expectations (for example tasks, cleaning, diary entries, to-do lists), social demands and even sometimes consumer advertising.

Reactance theory explains that such expectations (or demands) threatens and reduces a person's own perceived sense of freedom. For example, a negative reactance occurs when a person feels that something is taking away their freedom and potential opportunity of exercising freewill. This is especially true for some people when the demand is mundane as it reduces the person's liberty and options to do more pleasant and exciting things.

Some individuals are naturally high in reactance. Not always, but usually the people who experience reactance often have a creative personality. This makes sense because their personality trait for creativity is wanting to explore more meaningful and exciting endeavours associated with their interests so it is natural for the brain to have a reactance to mundane boring tasks such as flushing a toilet, putting a washing on, emptying a bin or putting the dishes away.

How to overcome reactance?

The best strategy for people who have reactance behaviour is to tell themselves, *"You don't have to, but ..."* and then suggest what may need done. Another example could be telling yourself (or others), *"You can try doing x but can always stop if you want to."* It seems by giving yourself the option of opting out reduces the reactance and actually frees you up to do the thing you've been avoiding. Using this self-talk with things such as the one-minute guide can help people overcome reactance. For example, *"I will try and do X after lunch, I can stop whenever I like, but even if I try it for one minute then I've done something productive"* can be very effective.

The one-minute guide

You would be surprised how much can be done within one minute.

Wipe down a surface	Clear a worktop	Put mail into a folder	Make a bed
Brush a floor	Clear as much rubbish into a bin within a minute	Dust something	Hang up some clothes/jackets
Wash a couple of things in the sink	Empty a bin	Put the washing machine on	Personal care: cut nails/brush teeth/ brush hair /wash self
Put away some plates/cups	Wipe a mirror/ window with a wipe	Hang a washing up	Wipe inside the microwave
Put away some shoes	Put keys/purse phone chargers where they belong – or make a permanent place for them	Put belongings away (hair dryer/ books etc.)	Tidy up for one minute before bed: tv remote away, cups away etc

You could implement the one-minute guide when the kettle is boiling, when there is a TV advert on or when you are waiting on someone. You could complete five of the above tasks in five minutes.

Obviously you would wish to do more than one minute. The idea behind the one-minute strategy is to get you started, and once started it is likely you will continue for a period of time. Some days one minute may be enough due to energy levels, other days you may do more. However, by developing this strategy you will be as productive as you possible can be on any given day.

Don't focus on the overall thing that needs done, just focus on starting. Tell yourself, *"I can stop this at any time, it is just starting that is important."*

There is no point trying to micromanage things. The best thing is to move in a direction that is positive for you; better to get started and improve rather than not starting at all. For example, instead of saying you want to lose two stone of weight (the final goal), you could change it to *"I am going to make decisions which will help me lose weight."* Eventually you will make enough micro-decisions which will result in the major difference you seek. Use this approach for other areas of your life you wish to improve. For example, you could tell yourself *"I am going to make decisions which will help me with having a clean house… keep me clean and healthy."* You could even combine this with the one-minute rule. For example, you could say *"For the next minute I am going to do something which will help me have a clean house."* If you do this often you will be surprised how much you will get done.

If time management is too difficult for you, try breaking your day into chunks. This will help you plan in your head better. For example, you could chunk your day with things like before lunch, after lunch, before dinner, after dinner and then before bedtime. That way you can tell yourself *"After lunch I will do something in the house,"* or *"After dinner I will do some housework."* This way you are not committing yourself to specific goals, instead, you are committing yourself to micro-improvements that will help you the most. For example, you could tell yourself that you will try doing something, even for one minute, in relation to something before a certain time of the day.

If you are a person who likes downtime, why not try and do some mundane tasks by a certain point of the day? Once the mundane tasks have been completed you can relax and enjoy downtime without guilt. If this appeals to you, your brain will likely focus to get the mundane tasks done quickly to allow itself to relax and enjoy your interests.

Themed days can help people who do like some structure but not micromanaged. Themed days are days of the week that you use to complete certain things. For example, Tuesday could be open letters day, Thursday could be cleaning day and so on. You don't have to do these tasks the whole day, just allocate some time during the day, even if it is just to apply the one-minute rule for those days when you feel up to it.

The key to daily organisation is habit. Get into the habit of putting things away properly. For example, hanging up keys, putting letters away and so on all help build habits. It might be annoying having to take an extra minute or two to put things away properly but your future self will be happy you did so, especially when you are rushing to find things.

Procrastination around household tasks

You may struggle with procrastination around household tasks with things such as putting dishes away, putting clothes away, emptying overflowing bins and so on. Over time you may have become tolerant of an unclean and unkept house. It doesn't need to be like this as you deserve better. The information below will hopefully help you overcome procrastination.

There is no strict rule saying you have to hold onto things. Be good to yourself, you don't have to keep old furniture, clothes, and belongings just for the sake of it. Why not treat yourself to new things and furniture?

Try practising the one-minute rule, it will help you with household tasks.

Instead of perceiving tasks that place a demand on you, change the mindset of tasks into games. For example, *"I am going to try and clean this better than last time... how quickly can I brush this for?... I'd be number 1 if this was a sport."* Remember, the best advice is to tell yourself, *"I can stop at any time I choose."* You will be surprised at how much you can get done knowing you can stop whenever you wish.

If you have difficulty procrastinating, try saying "NOW I AM GOING TO START in 5,4,3,2,1..." and then just start what you've been avoiding. Remember, it is all about getting started. Don't worry about doing the thing to a high standard, a bad first start is better than no start.

If you do procrastinate, just tell yourself, *"All I need to do to resolve this situation is just move some muscles."* Completion of most daily tasks is a result of simple motor movement, the problem is we overthink them. We distort the effort needed. For example, if the sink is full of dishes, instead of telling yourself "*I need to do all those dishes,*" change the self-talk to "*What muscle movement do I need to clean that? I simply need to just move some arms, move hands and that will wash the dishes.*" It really is that easy. You have the ability to carry out these simple motor movements, so just tell yourself so.

The same principle can be applied to all things you've been avoiding. For example, putting the rubbish out is basically walking and carrying something. Wiping a window is moving your arm. Updating a diary is simply writing with a pen. Don't over think, just tell yourself to act out the basic motor movements for the things you have been avoiding.

Sometimes it is best imagining what the end result should be and then plan the steps that is needed to get there. This allows you to understand the actions needed and helps you be mindful of the wider context of things.

A timer can help you focus on a task. However, some people may feel this is too formal. Instead, you can use other mediums that will help your brain understand time. For example, maybe listening to some songs or a music album will help you understand how long a task is taking. This will help you keep to the time you want to spend on tasks. It could also be a radio show, an audiobook, podcast, or some motivational speaking which will help you understand the duration of time. This may help you justify the time you are spending on a task as you will be getting some sort of benefit. Remember, focus on the positives.

Too much stuff. Some people tend to hang onto things that start taking over space in the house. Maybe once a month put items you have no use for (clothes, belongings and so on) into a donation box. Once the box is full you could donate to a charity shop or recycle centre. This will help you reclaim much needed space while doing a good thing for other people or the environment. Only keep what you need and really want. More stuff usually means more clutter and therefore more anxiety.

Home organisation should be functional. For example, how often do you forget where you have put things such as keys, phone or bags? If you give things a specific place within your home then they won't be lost all the time. Ensure everyday items has a specific place within your home. You need to be disciplined to make it work. Even when you can't be bothered force yourself to put things away properly. You could use the one-minute guidance to put things where they belong as you know your future self will be thankful you took the time to organise.

When tidying up you can use the ten-second guide. The idea is to try and put things away within ten seconds as this will help avoid procrastination. If ten seconds is too short, you could make it twenty seconds or one minute.

Anxiety

As anxiety is worrying about the unknown or lack of clarity, then it makes sense to plan in advance if possible. Planning helps bring stability and this will generally help reduce anxiety.

A lot of the time there is anxiety due to the difficulty of imagining how something will stop or end. Factor this into your planning. Just by knowing how or why something can be stopped will help the brain from over worrying. For example, you could tell yourself *"This thing will be finished by no later than x o'clock, I then get to go home and relax."*

Try and have a back-up plan should things not go as expected. This could even be something like *"If things become too intense, I will leave and go home."* Or having a written plan with you about what to do if you are too anxious. Just by allowing your brain to visualise something other than the worst-case scenario may help prevent your brain from fearing the worse.

Avoid leaving the house late if you need to be somewhere for a specific time. Being late will make you even more anxious.

If you feel the sensation of anxiety coming on it may help to start focusing on your breathing. There are various relaxing breathing exercises that can be found through an internet search.

Be aware of your sensory sensitivities. Is the source of your anxiety caused by overexposure to things such as noises, lights, smells and so on? If so, try and make the environment more relaxed for yourself. Things such as headphones, sun caps, glasses and comfort breaks may help avoid sensory overload.

You could also be anxious due to the clothes you are wearing. Wear comfortable clothing.

Your anxiety may also be a result of you not having enough to eat or drink, or the need to go to the toilet. Try and remind yourself about these needs throughout the day. It is okay to set reminders for such things.

After experiencing anxiety, give yourself permission to rest when you can otherwise you will become worn out. Be sure to allow yourself time within the week (and maybe each day) the opportunity to relax and enjoy some of your interests. You need to ensure you have the opportunity to do the things you enjoy.

Be aware of an over-reliance with things like alcohol and drugs. These behaviours are often used when trying to cope and they can become problematic quickly. If you are unsure about your use with such substances seek advice from a professional or someone you trust.

If you are anxious about something coming up, try and focus on the positives of it. Even if there is nothing relatively positive, ask yourself, will your future self be happy you went through such an activity. This can be useful for things such as appointments with a health care professional.

Developing better self-esteem and wellbeing

Don't be so hard on yourself with critical self-talk. What would you say to another autistic person? Would you be supportive? If yes, then why not be supportive towards yourself? Positive self-talk leads to progression and self-improvements.

Your brain will learn differently compared with others. This means you may learn things differently. Comparing yourself with others only leads to jealousy, frustration or hubristic pride. Compare yourself with yourself.

If you want or expect something to happen, and it's not happening, speak up and tell people about your expectations. Give them the context of why it is important and remember don't assume people know what you are thinking. Be specific. For example, don't just state the issue, *"I can't eat that."* Instead, give clarity, for example *"The texture makes me feel sick, that is why I can't eat that."* Again, don't assume people will automatically know what you are thinking.

Frustration often arises as a result of a build-up of little things over the day. In isolation, these little things can be seen as trivial, however over a full day they can cause burnout. Factor self-care throughout the day to avoid the little things becoming too much.

Supporting sensory sensitivities

Remember, each day is different and your tolerances to sensory sensitivities may vary. Therefore, it may be helpful to plan ahead if you have to go somewhere. For example, sunglasses, a hat, earplugs, headphones, a stimming fidget toy and various other things may help. It is good to go to places prepared, but don't pack everything, just pack what is practically needed.

Sometimes it is best to do an assessment of the environment you are going to, or even when you are there. When you are there look for any potential things that may overwhelm you. For example, when going somewhere like a restaurant, don't sit under bright lights if this is too much. Be careful of being close to doorbells, hand dryers, machinery, speakers, alarms and so on.

You may like fashion, but if the clothes you are wearing are overwhelming is it really worth it? Once you discover the clothes that you feel comfortable in, such as the texture, the fitting, the fabric and so on, you can then be creative and accessorise these comfortable feeling clothes to look better if you so wish.

Be aware of your energy levels as they could be linked to your sensory sensitivities. Are you being overexposed to unnecessary stimuli, is there something that could help reduce this from what you have read? If so, do something about it and see if it helps. Sometimes recording things in a journal or diary may help you identify patterns.

You may have a restricted diet, just be mindful of eating enough calories. It is best for health to eat a variety of foods. If you would like to increase variety why not try experimenting? Introduce new foods in a way that is interesting. For example, what is it you like about the foods and drinks you currently take? Are there similar foods that have the same texture, taste and look that you haven't tried yet? You may be happy with the foods you already eat, but you may also discover foods that you will really enjoy too. Introduce change slowly. For example, one small bite size to begin with.

Keeping clean

People are going to judge you by how clean and tidy you are. Being messy and unclean informs other people that you are unkept, untidy and not well organised. This may impact on your ability to develop and keep relationships with people whom you wish to do so. For example, friends at class, at work, at a sports club, a hobby, an event or even a date.

There may be some personal grooming tasks that may be difficult for you and this is why you have avoided doing them. However, if personal grooming needs are left for a prolonged period of time they will become much more difficult to overcome. For example, not brushing teeth will result in more visits to the dentist, not washing may result in hospitalisation and poor hygiene could mean less opportunities for meaningful relationships and employment.

Take self-care seriously. Washing yourself, your hair, your clothes and cutting your nails on a regular basis are all important. Only a small time is needed for such small tasks if they are undertaken on a regular basis. Even using the one-minute guide may be enough to undertake such personal grooming needs.

There may be reasons why some of these things are difficult for you. If you are unsure how to approach such personal grooming tasks, or how often, ask someone you trust by using their knowledge as a reference point and develop a structure that works for you. Even watching how other people undertake such activities can help you develop strategies that may help.

If you are unsure if you are untidy or have poor grooming skills, ask someone you trust for feedback and advice.

You may be reluctant to buy new clothes or shoes as the ones that you wear are comfortable. You have to get the balance right between what is comfortable and what is clean. For example, trainers may be comfortable but if they are dirty and have holes it may be time to purchase a new pair. You can still have the comfort you desire with something new, for example you could purchase the same trainers (or similar) as you had before, this way they will feel similar but are clean and tidy. The same could be for all sorts of clothing such as socks, underwear, bedding, towels, trousers, t-shirts, skirts, tops, jackets and so on.

Going for an autism diagnosis

A lot of autistic people tell of their relief to finally be diagnosed as this provides and explanation for their life experiences in a way that makes sense to them. For some other autistic people, they may have been diagnosed before they were ready. The diagnosis may have come as a surprise and it may take time to adjust. However, mostly all people say they would rather know they are autistic than not know. This is why it is good to hear how other autistic people speak about their experiences.

By communicating with other autistic people (online, watching YouTube videos or reading blogs and books) you will be able to understand autistic culture better. This will help you understand if you are autistic or not. If you are autistic you will identify with what other autistic people say. Be sure to try and listen from various autistic people because no two autistic people are the same. Having a better understanding of autism and your own autistic needs will mean you will be more confident when pursuing a formal diagnosis if you wish to do so.

Conclusion

Hopefully there has been some strategies that you may find useful.

Remember, very rarely does anything happen perfectly the first time. You are developing yourself and improvements take time. Be kind and patient with yourself, in time things will become easier.

You may want to read appendix 2 to understand some ways people can help support autistic needs as this may help you articulate what supports may help you the most.

References

1. Peterson, Jordan B., et al. "Page 246." 12 Rules for Life: An Antidote to Chaos, Vintage Canada, Toronto, 2020. In this book Jordan Peterson heavily attributes this approach through work of the psychologist Carl Rodgers.

Appendix 2
Providing sensitive autistic support

This chapter explains strategies that may help you provide sensitive support for autistic people. There are no strategies that are specifically for mental health. This is because autism is not a mental health issue. Instead, it is a lack of sensitive support that often results in poor mental health for autistic people. The best way to help autistic people overcome poor mental health is to first ensure their autistic needs are supported.

Autistic attention

Although autistic people may show extreme attention with certain interests, such interests are often limited to one or two things at any one time, often meaning the person may be missing the wider context of what is unfolding around them.

Neurotypical people can shift their attention within multiple contexts. For example, during social interactions neurotypical people: (1) look at facial expressions, (2) focus on the word context, (3) listen for pitch and range as well as, (4) using problem-solving skills to try and understand what the person is communicating and why. However, some autistic people may only be able to pay attention to one or two elements of the social interaction meaning they may struggle to understand the overall context of what is being communicated. Being aware of narrowed focus and attention can help develop a better understanding of why some autistic people may struggle in certain environments. Remember, single focused attention is not a choice for autistic people, it is often how the autistic brain functions (more left hemisphere dominant).

Attention is a finite resource, and after intense periods the brain needs to relax. Daily tasks (big and small) for autistic people can often drain resources needed for attention. Factor in rest breaks.

Make the distinction between what is currently happening compared to what is about to happen [1]. For example, when neurotypical people tell someone something is about to happen (going out, or going for a shower), they usually mean the process of building up to the event that is about to unfold. For example, getting shoes on before going out or starting to take clothes off prior to entering a shower. However, often the autistic brain will take such statements literally, for example, the autistic person may suddenly walk out the house with no shoes on, or go into the shower with all their clothes on. This is why it is important to make the distinction between what is currently happening compared to the process of events that should happen before the activity begins. For example, "*before we go out, it is usually a good idea to put on footwear*".

It can be hard for neurotypical people to always communicate the context and processes. A helpful hint is once you have said what you said, always ask yourself, "*Do I need to give more clarity and context?*" So, say you said the following statement to an autistic person "*We are about to go out,*" you could follow this up with "*So this means we should collect the footwear we need, organise the …*[and so on]" as this helps the autistic person to focus on the next practical step and develop a wider understanding of the context.

Allow time for the autistic brain to adjust to new environments and transitions. Visual aids can help the autistic person focus their attention on important changes and transitions in the environment.

Discussing different subject matters interchangeably can be very confusing for some autistic people. The attention to focus on one topic may just be enough, so when other ideas and concepts are added without the proper adjustment time some autistic people may experience distress. Also, it can also be confusing when people talk interchangeably between past, present and future [1].

Narrowed focus and attention may result in delayed processing for some people. For example, long after a social interaction the autistic brain may still be processing all the individual components (tone, words, body language, meaning, emotion). Therefore, it may take the person more time to fully understand the wider context of the interaction (two brain hemisphere function R-L-R). The same can be said for emotions.

During a social interaction the autistic person may not have fully understood the emotions that were exchanged. The brain may need time to process all the individual parts of the interaction before fully understanding the emotions. This can explain why some autistic people often experience intense emotional reactions well after the social interaction has taken place. This can be quite confusing for some people as the delayed processing of the emotion is not in the context of where it originally happened. For example, say something happened at school or work, maybe the person isn't able to understand the full context due to a limited attention span at the time, but can eventually process it in an environment they feel comfortable in such as their home.

Supporting communication

Communication consists of multiple parts. For example, spoken words, gestures, tone of voice, facial expressions, emotion and intention are needed for communication. However, autistic people are often only able to focus attention on one or two elements of communication at any one time. However, all autistic people can communicate if the right support is provided in a caring and understanding way. The more pleasant the communication the more likely the person will engage.

If possible seek guidance on the preferred way the person communicates. For example, ask the person, a family member or professional for advice. If needed use visuals, pictures, photographs, videos, objects of reference and/or the use of written word if needed. The person may prefer to communicate by letters, emails, texts, telephone, shorter meetings or longer meetings, all of which should be supported if possible.

Some other people may need to be supported with augmented communication. Augmentative communication is when you add something to speech. For example, sign language, pictures, gestures and body language all add to speech. Some other people may need Alternative Communication. This is where a system or device is used instead of speech. The need for such provision is often assessed by a professional.

Autistic people will often communicate more if they are allowed to focus their attention on something which is important to them. Use interests and hobbies to build communication skills, be creative. The more the person engages with communication the better as this will help support non-verbal skills such as turn taking, joint attention and reciprocity.

Autistic people often take what is said literally. This is why you should say what you mean and mean what you say with autistic people. This can be very difficult for neurotypical people because they often use humour, sarcasm and exaggeration when communicating. A good way to ensure you are supporting autistic people sensitively is to always explain the context of what you are saying. This will ensure you have been sensitive without being self-conscious of saying the wrong thing. A helpful tip is to check what you said makes sense. For example, if you say to someone *"I'm away to the shops,"* you may initially think they know you will be back shortly. However, you haven't said when, or if you will even be back. Again, always clarify what you said by explaining the context, *"I'm going to the shops for milk"*, you then want to clarify the wider context so you then say, *"I will be back, and no later than x o'clock."*

If you mean something literally, tell the person *"I meant that literally."* If you have said something which was sarcastic, funny or exaggerated then just summarise that to the person while giving the wider context. For example, say you said, *"I could eat my own body weight,"* clarify it with something like, *"What I really meant was I am really hungry."* It is hard to always try and watch what you say but by clarifying the intended context is often enough for the autistic person to understand what was communicated.

Remember, autistic people may process emotions differently. A lot of autistic people comment how emotive language can create emotional affect. Therefore, try and not use strong emotive words if possible. Also, try and not criticise, even if you are only trying to help. If possible, use positive phrases such as *"It may help if… it would be good if… I think this would help better because…"*, and then give the context why.

Remember, autistic people will often have their attention fixed on one or two things, so using abstract language, jumping between subjects, or explaining things with complex language, abstract ideas, abbreviations, jargon and non-literal language may confuse the person.

Offer regular opportunities for the person to engage. For example, you could say *"Is there anything that I said that has worried you or confused you… is there anything that you want me to clarify… would you like me to go over that again… is there anything you would like to ask me about this?"*

There is a way to help overcome confusion around communication. Peterson and Rodgers explain there are three points to follow [2]:

1. Listen to what is being said.
2. Summarise back to the person the overall meaning of what you think they said. For example, you could say *"Am I right in understanding you mean… so I can understand this a bit better, you said… but now you are saying this… why is there a difference?"*
3. After you have summarised what you thought the person was saying, listen to what the person has to say. They will either say *"Yes, you've summarised that well… exactly… yes, that is what I was trying to say* [or something to that effect]". If the person doesn't think you've summarised the meaning of what they said they will likely say things such as *"Not quite… what I meant was this… it's more like this…"* This is good because they have now told you what they were thinking.

If the person you are supporting or caring for is non-verbal, I would suggest adopting the approach called Intensive Interaction. Instead of trying to explain the approach in detail it is better to direct you to the free internet resources for learning and understanding this approach. I would recommend an internet search of Phoebe Caldwell as this will provide you with all the information needed to start the approach.

Intensive Interaction builds rapport and trust and the results are often staggering and heart-warming. Often people feel self-conscious when trying the approach initially, but after some practice people soon realise how easy and engaging the approach is. If you are going to support someone with the approach I would encourage you to be authentic, always engage with warmth and have a willingness to connect.

Supporting social and emotional understanding

Often autistic people will struggle to imagine how a social event may unfold. Therefore, help the person develop a mental understanding of what may happen and what they can do within such events.

Firstly, always explain the context about the social event. Explain the who, where, what, when, why and how if needed. Also, explain how it will likely finish. Don't give absolutes, sometimes unexpected things happen. Try and use statements such as *"It is likely this will happen... you will probably be asked this... this generally tends to happen."* Over time this helps the person develop generalised concepts of context for fluid situations.

Make expectations clear about what may be expected from the person. Don't assume the person will automatically know or understand.

You may want to use visuals to help the person understand better. Pictures, photographs, magazines, videos and so on may help the person develop a mental image of what may socially unfold. Also, try and keep the visuals authentic, try and use actual photographs and videos as much as you can.

Social Stories, comic strips and story writing can all help the person understand what will likely happen within a social situation. Other visuals can help too. For example, thought bubbles, drawings and role play can all help develop concepts of what may unfold socially.

Recordings (photographs, videos, drawings and audio clips) of an event can also be played back later to help the person process and understand what had taken place. Help the person focus on the positives of the experiences as this will likely help them feel less anxious when attending similar events or activities in the future.

The use of watching TV, films, YouTube and TikTok may all help the person understand what may unfold in future social events. Be careful when using abstract visual information as the autistic person may have difficulty generalising. For example, if you used a TV show to demonstrate attending the dentist, the person may not enter the local dental surgery as they will think it is the wrong dentist. This is because they think they should be attending the same one they saw on TV. Only use visuals if you believe they will help the person, don't just use them for the sake of it.

Attending groups around special interests could help develop social skills naturally.

Allow extra processing time, especially in new social situations. Autistic people often focus on one thing at a time, so somewhere new will mean a different layout, different people, different social norms and different sensory experiences. Allow time to settle, stim, or talk about interests for a short while when entering in a new social context as this may help them relax.

Regularly check how the person is coping, for example *"Are you feeling okay to keep going … would you like a break?"* Even if the person says no, it is often good to factor in some comfort breaks to avoid overwhelming the person.

Consider the times of social interactions for things like meetings or appointments. For example, if it's early how difficult will it be for the person to travel with things like rush hour traffic? Other people may be too tired in the afternoons. Can adjustments be made to times and or venues?

If possible, have a familiar person support the autistic person when in a potential difficult situation. Just by having a supporting person available is often enough to empower the autistic person to engage positively in difficult situations. The same applies for having an exit strategy. Work with the person and identify a way of knowing when too much is too much. Again, this will help the autistic person have the confidence to engage as they know they will be less likely to experience a situation that gets out of their control. It is similar to trying something if you knew you couldn't get hurt, you would likely try it. Having a safe person, and/or exit strategy really helps the person understand they will not be subject to unnecessary pain or ridicule and they will therefore be more likely to try new things.

Supporting planning and organising (executive function skills)

Autistic people can struggle with executive functioning skills such as planning, using working memory, generalising, decision-making, time-management, predicting what will likely happen, problem-solving, change and transitions.

Having difficulty with executive functioning skills often results in autistic people implementing their own rules and routines to install order to make things more predictable. This naturally gives the impression that autistic people are rule-based, inflexible and resistant to any change.

Hyper focus enables autistic people to excel at some things, but as all the attention is on one or two things means it is very hard for them to change their attention to other things.

Develop a clear understanding of the difference between routines and structure. A routine is a certain way of doing something every time. Structure is different as it allows a sense of predictability while allowing a degree of flexibility. Support aids such as now & next cards, schedules, choice boards and back up plans can all help the person understand a change better. These supports help provide the predictability the person craves but allows scope for things to change without the person experiencing unnecessary distress.

Some people may prefer clear and well-defined plans and systems. Others may feel intimidated by perceiving such demands with things such as diaries, schedules, to-do lists and planners. Other people may need supported with informal strategies (discussed in appendix one). Only use support aids if you believe they will work.

Often autistic people may become so singularly focused on one or two things that they may not pay attention to the other areas of their lives. If needed, point out the areas that an autistic person may be neglecting. An example could be personal hygiene. It is best to explain why it is important for them.

Try and make any unknowns more known. It is often the ambiguous, less well defined or not yet clarified that causes distress for autistic people. Sometimes it is easier for people to mentally process something they don't like compared with endless worry and anxiety about the things that are unknown.

Sometimes it may be helpful to demonstrate what the change involves, for example maybe you could put on the ear defenders, you put on the jumper, you sit in the chair and so on. Model what needs to be done.

Always try and explain the context. For example, who you are, who are the other people, what are your roles, what will likely happen, when will you know something has started and when something will likely finish. Give logical information which will help the person remember, organise and plan better. Visuals can help structure activities with a clear beginning, middle and end.

Understand it may be difficult for an autistic person to take a different approach to something once they have been shown how to previously do a task in a specific way. Spend time reassuring the person about possible changes or what is happening. Always explain the context and don't assume the person will know or feel comfortable with the change. A lot of people will just say they are okay because they are either anxious or are afraid of admitting potential failure.

Change can be extremely difficult. Often people need to know what is coming next as it provides them with comfort. Not only do people need time to process changes, but they will also need time to make the mental adjustments required to go through the change [1]. If possible, give information in advance. Double appointments, extra transition time, extra breaks and even things like a time reminder could help some people build up to events.

Break activities into smaller steps as this may prevent overloading the person. Visual supports could help greatly in this area. To-do lists, now & next, job cards, timetables, agendas, social stories and various others can all be helpful to support understanding of what is about to happen.

Time management may be difficult for some people. Timers, watches, mini-alarms, units of time such as a song or TV programme could help some people understand concepts of time better.

If something does need to change, inform the person of the logic of why the change is needed. Don't use generic social language such as *"That's life, it wasn't that important anyway, you'll be fine."* Support the person to understand the changes, use visual information if you believe this will help.

If possible, provide the person with a summary of what was done or already completed. This will help them process what they have already achieved and what still needs to be done.

Supporting sensory sensitivities

Autistic people experience sensory sensitivities. This will mean different things for different people. Some people may be oversensitive to things such as noise, lights, smells, tastes and textures. For example, sensory sensitivities may occur when a person is exposed to:

- Overhead lights, fluorescent lights, sunlight, shiny surfaces, flashing lights and certain colours. Also, patterns in clothes, carpets, wallpaper and furniture may be distracting or overwhelming.
- Noises such as hand-dryers, hairdryers, white noise (hoovers, machinery), background noise (chit-chat), bells, alarms or sudden noises.
- Food smells, perfumes, deodorants, toiletries, air fresheners and potentially anything fragranced.

- Tastes such as certain foods and liquids.
- Textures and sensations on the skin such as clothing, tags, socks and shoes. Food textures may restrict diet. Temperature regulation for things like the weather, rain, heat or the cold. Touch from others, particularly if not expected. Grooming needs such washing, hair washing, teeth brushing, haircuts and cutting nails.
- Interoception needs (the internal sensations of the body) such as hunger, thirst, toiletry needs and feelings. People may have difficulty knowing when they are hungry, thirsty or full. People may have difficulty feeling the sensation of personal care needs. Some others may have difficulty with their emotional regulation.
- Sensory motor movement. Most autistic people enjoy seeking out sensory motor movement. Some people may prefer swings, trampolines, bike-riding or going for drives. Some others may engage in repetitive self-stimulating movement such as rocking, hand flapping, biting, bending, jumping, tiptoe walking or bending muscle and limbs.

Remember, narrowed attention may only be on one sensory stimulus at any one time, therefore too much sensory stimulation could be overwhelming and distressing.

Everyone will have their own sensory sensitivities. Some people may avoid certain sensory experiences, others may seek out the sensory experiences that others avoid. If possible, ask the person if they have sensory preferences and what you can do to support these. If you can't ask the person, try and understand what sensory experience the person is either seeking or avoiding. Just by mirroring what the person is doing may give you an indication of what the person may be experiencing or seeking themselves.

If sensory sensitivities are too difficult to understand research the subject. There are excellent free resources on the internet including YouTube videos from autistic people explaining what sensory sensitivities are like.

Consider if adjustments could be made to help with sensory overload. Could earplugs, headphones, sensory de-stressors, fidget toys, distractors and comfort breaks be made available?

Is there time factored into the person's day to help them regulate their sensory levels and sensory motor system?

Always consider the impact of sensory experiences when going somewhere. Consider if the venue, environment or time is likely to be difficult. For example, rush hour traffic, busy times and what the person may have experienced before arriving can all impact on sensory sensitivities.

Consider that a person may be experiencing overload when attending somewhere new. For example, the sensory overload of changing their routine, the transport to get to the venue, the amount of social interaction experienced so far. Try and help avoid overload if possible. The person might need some time to regulate before being able to effectively engage.

Give information as to what the environment may be like and plan ahead with support strategies. This could be requesting double appointment slots to help the person adjust, or request a room with no overhead lights, or a quiet room.

Any written information, documents and display boards could be sensory sensitive. Make things obvious, use borders and don't overload with information or use overemotional content.

If you want to introduce new foods, do so in a way that is interesting for the person, for example, can interests and passions be used? If a person likes certain textures and tastes, try replicating that with other foods, be creative. Introduce change slowly, even if this means you putting one spoonful on your plate so the person starts to see the foods, and then over time you could eventually put a spoonful on their plate and so on.

Encourage the use of clothes that will not cause sensory overload. You can fashion comfort clothes if needed.

Remember, sensory issues are often magnified when the person is tired.

One page reflection box

The one-page reflection box is a good way of thinking what supports may be helpful to a person in any given situation. The reflection box makes you think holistically about what supports may be useful and why, or why an autistic person may be struggling with a specific issue.

The best way to think about using the reflection box is to ask yourself, does the person have any challenges with these? If so, use some of the identified strategies throughout this book to help support the person. Also, you could ask yourself, does the person have any strengths in these areas? If so, use these strengths to help work around some of the difficulties the person is experiencing.

Figure 2: One page autism reflection box.

Communicating	Social & emotional understanding	Executive function skills and attention	Sensory sensitivities
Non-speech communication – body language, eye-gaze, body positioning.	Empathy – seeing others point of view.	Organisation.	Sensory seeker – hyper/sensory avoider – hyposensitive.
Receptive communication – whether this is using specific objects, generalised objects, gestures, photographs, drawing, formal signs – such as Makaton, symbols, speech or written language.	Understanding social norms, such as reciprocity, unwritten rules, manners, humour.	Attention, focus and special interests.	Differences in processing sounds/noises.

Communicating	Social & emotional understanding	Executive function skills and attention	Sensory sensitivities
Expressive communication – whether this is using specific objects, generalised objects, gestures, photographs, drawing, formal signs – such as BSL/Makaton, symbols, speech or written language.	Understanding social situations, such as different roles, expectations or norms. Insensitive/ indifferent to others.	Motivation.	Differences in processing proprioception inputs – body awareness.
Echolalia – repeating specific noises, words or catchphrases which appear to have no significant meaning.	Social use of language. For example, what to say, who to say it to, Where and when to say it, Questions – too many/too few.	Planning/ initiative.	Differences in processing vestibular inputs – balance and movement.
Communicating feelings and emotions.	Poor joint attention. Lack of interaction/ interest in others.	Working memory.	Differences in processing visual inputs/filtering.
Communicating likes, preferences or choices.	Understanding/ respecting personal space.	Generalising/ understanding the wider context.	Differences in processing smells.
Communicating dislikes/ unhappiness.	Difficulty with relationships – either establishing or maintaining.	Problem-solving/ learning new skills.	Differences in processing tastes.
Communicating difficulties.	Understanding own emotions, and/or the emotions of others.	Predicting what will happen next, Outcomes/ consequences of actions.	Differences in processing touch.

Communicating	Social & emotional understanding	Executive function skills and attention	Sensory sensitivities
Starting/ending a communication effectively and/or appropriately. Developing two-way communication.	Over/underestimated emotional responses.	Understanding the context of situations/events.	Differences in pain tolerances.
Talking too much/too little.	Understanding motive/intent of others.	Difficulty with big/small changes and/or transitions.	Difficulty in regulating temperature/thirst/hunger.
Situational mutism.	Difficulty offering/asking for help.	Concept of time/time management.	Differences in reactions to thirst/hunger.
Engaging in reciprocal turn taking when communicating.	Inappropriate social behaviours, such as sharing too much information or too honest.	Decision making.	Distress towards physical changes in environment.

References

1. Lawson, Wendy. The Passionate Mind: How People with Autism Learn. Jessica Kingsley Publishers, 2011.
2. Peterson, Jordan B., et al. "Page 246." 12 Rules for Life: An Antidote to Chaos, Vintage Canada, Toronto, 2020. In this book Jordan Peterson heavily attributes this approach through work of the psychologist Carl Rodgers.

Appendix 3
Autism B Biochemistry Model

Figure 25 gives a more detailed explanation of the biochemical pathways likely involved with autism. The Figure visually highlights some of the complexity involved in such pathways explaining Autism B Theory. It is thought this visual may be useful to help readers should they wish to read or research more on the subject.

Figure 25: Detailed biochemical pathway explaining Autism B theory.

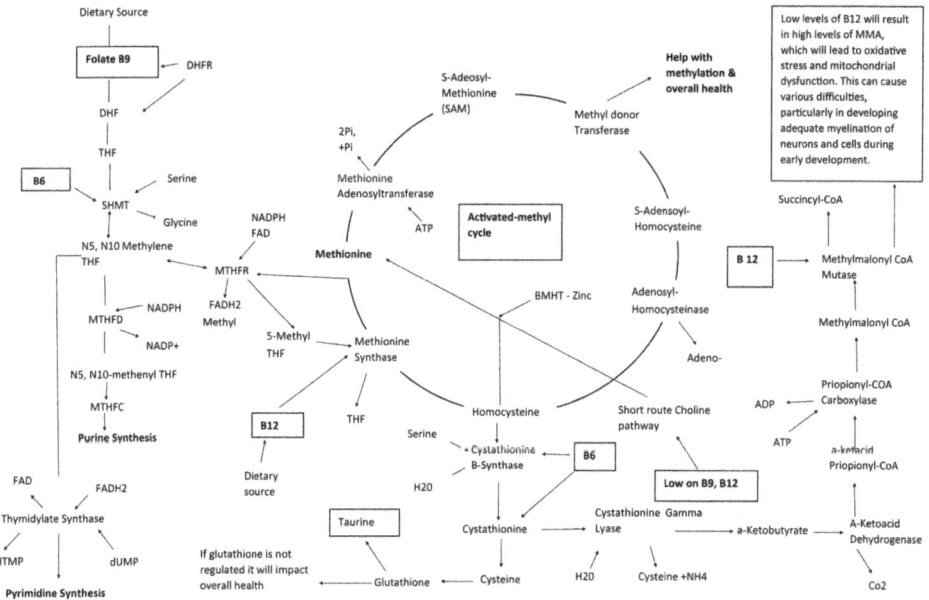

Appendix 4
Alexithymia

People with alexithymia have difficulty identifying and describing their emotional experiences. Some also have difficulty understanding the connections of feelings and the associated bodily sensations.

Some of the common features of alexithymia are:

- Difficulty identifying different feelings.
- Difficulty recognising facial communication in others.
- Difficulty understanding bodily sensations with emotions.
- Detached or hesitant connection to others.

Although multiple factors are thought to play a role in the development of alexithymia, theorists have mostly highlighted the contribution towards early atypical development.

Research varies, but high levels of alexithymia occur in approximately 10% of the population. There are some suggestions that alexithymia is connected to autism. Although alexithymia is not a core feature of autism, recent studies have found varying degrees of this trait (50 to 85%) of autistic people [1].

If the sensory motor stage of development (birth to two years) is atypical, then this will impact on the next stage of development; the emotional stage (two to three years). The emotional stage is often referred to as the terrible twos. It is as if all the emotions are trying to force their one-dimensional mode of being to be the only way the infant should act. The successful completion of the emotional stage is to have all the emotions regulated within the body. If there are sensory sensitivities, especially in relation to an under responsive sensory motor system, then this will likely result in interoception difficulty which will impact on the person's ability to regulate internal emotional feelings. This, coupled with an atypical myelinated Social Engagement System can explain why so many autistic people may have alexithymia.

Autistic people with alexithymia often have to pretend emotions to try and fit in socially. This pretend behaviour is called masking and it can often come at a cost. Eventually, the only emotions that will be familiar over time will be confusion, fear and anger.

Confusion about the mismatch of pretend behaviour and internal emotional feeling.

Fear of getting the pretend emotional behaviour wrong.

Anger for having to pretend to feel and act in a way that is not meaningful just so they can fit in socially.

The autistic disposition of sensory sensitivities, social communication differences and alexithymia will mean some autistic people will have additional barriers when trying to develop relationships. The inability to express emotions and bodily sensations may result in feelings of loneliness and isolation which are all markers for developing poor mental health. It is essential that any person or professional wanting to support an autistic person will need to understand that it may be likely the autistic person may struggle to talk about their emotional experiences and associated bodily sensations.

There is a wide range of resources that can help autistic people in relation to internal bodily emotion awareness. Work by Peter Levine, Antonio Damasio, Stephen Porges and Debs Dana are good sources of practical knowledge in relation to developing better interoception awareness (internal body). The book Healing Trauma, by Peter Levine has very practical guidance for developing better internal awareness.

References

1. Poquérusse, J., Pastore, L., Dellantonio, S., & Esposito, G. (2018). Alexithymia and Autism Spectrum Disorder: A Complex Relationship. Frontiers in psychology, 9, 1196. https://doi.org/10.3389/fpsyg.2018.0cognitive96

Appendix 5
Synaesthesia and Irlen Syndrome

Synaesthesia and Irlen syndrome are two different things. Both are more prevalent in the autistic population.

Synaesthesia

Synaesthesia is a condition in which the stimulation of one sense somehow stimulates unrelated sensory or cognitive pathways at the same time. Many people are not aware they have synaesthesia. Some people, but not everyone, consider synaesthesia to be a gift that allows them to see the world in a rich and unique way. Synaesthesia can enhance cognitive abilities such as creativity and memory. Some famous people with synaesthesia include Vincent van Gogh, Lady Gaga, Billy Joel and Pharrell Williams.

Examples of synaesthesia are:

- When someone hears music they may actually see patterns of colour.
- Another form of synaesthesia joins objects such as letters, shapes, numbers, or people's names with a sensory perception such as a smell, colour, or flavour. For example, *"There is yellow Stephen... there is blue 5... There is triangle Mark."*
- Sounds may be linked to colour. For example, *"There is the purple train (the noise of a train)... there is the pink bark (dog barking)."*
- Some people may be able to taste letters. For example, *"The sweet m."*
- Ordinary sequences (the days of the week) are associated with personalities or genders. For example: *"Man Monday... female Tuesday... moody Friday."*

There are literally dozens of different types of synaesthesia and many people can have more than one type. Some types of synaesthesia are more common than others. Grapheme-colour synaesthesia (coloured letters) or chromesthesia (music in colours) appear to be more prevalent.

Grapheme colour synaesthesia

Grapheme colour synaesthesia is one of the most common. It occurs when letters and numbers are associated with colours.

Chromesthesia (sometimes known as sound synaesthesia)

Chromesthesia is about sound and colour. It occurs when certain sounds trigger someone to see colours, brightness, shapes, tastes and smells.

Spatial sequence synaesthesia

Spatial sequence synaesthesia involves mentally seeing numbers or numerical sequences as points in space (close or far away). For example, 1998 may be distant to 1992, January before July, and Monday sequenced before Tuesday.

Auditory-tactile synaesthesia

Auditory-tactile synaesthesia is when hearing a sound activates sensations in different parts of the body.

Ordinal linguistic personification

Ordinal linguistic personification is the personalisation of sequences such as days, months and letters. For example, the number 2 might represent a female, and the letter P could mean angry man.

Misophonia

Misophonia is triggered by certain sounds. The experience of mysophonia is that of anger, hate and disgust.

Lexical-gustatory synaesthesia

Lexical-gustatory synaesthesia occurs when certain words trigger taste sensations.

The cause of synaesthesia is unknown. Some scientists believe that synaesthesia results from crossed wiring in the brain during early atypical development. The explanation for synaesthesia is that neurons and synapses are supposed to be contained within one sensory system within the brain, but for some reason, within synaesthesia certain neurons will atypically connect to other parts of the brain. As highlighted within Autism B Theory, some neurons will connect to neighbouring neurons due to atypical myelination therefore possibly explaining the extra connectivity needed for synaesthesia.

Irlen syndrome

Irlen syndrome and synaesthesia are two different things, although some autistic people may have both.

Irlen syndrome (also referred to as Meares-Irlen syndrome, scotopic sensitivity syndrome, and visual stress) is a perceptual processing difference. It is not an eye problem; it's the brain's ability to process visual information.

Irlen syndrome can present differently for each individual. Here are some behaviours associated with Irlen Syndrome:

- Looking in short glances.
- Finger flicking.
- Poor eye contact.
- Rubbing, pushing on eyes.
- Fascinated by colours and patterns of light.
- Sensitive to specific lights.
- Poor motor coordination: clumsy, poor at sports, poor depth-perception.
- Objects are blurry, moving, changing, and can often disappear.
- Difficulties with depth perception make things like steps, and stairs difficult.

- Difficulty with reading. Words may appear to be blurry, moving, or disappear which makes following lines on a page and reading difficult.
- Difficulty with writing. There will often be unequal spacing, letter size, uneven writing and inconsistent spelling.
- Often complains of fatigue and repeated headaches. May also have an extreme sensitivity or preference towards certain colours.

It is still unclear what is the exact cause of Irlen syndrome.

Irlen Method for support

The Irlen Method assessment determines what colour of light the person responds to best and then glasses with lenses of the preferred colour are provided. The right colour of lens seems to dampen, and sometimes remove the difficulties associated with Irlen Syndrome. It is best to see an Irlen syndrome specialist to determine the right support. However, experimentation with colours can help develop some coping strategies while waiting on an assessment.

One method is to alter the lighting in one environment to see if it helps. For example, try using different coloured lightbulbs and see if any of them are preferred (for example yellow, red, blue, green, purple, brown, pink).

Try using coloured tinted sunglasses to see if there is a preference. There are some packs that are relatively cheap such as chromotherapy glasses.

Coloured reading strips (often called dyslexia or visual stress aids) can be very helpful. There are various coloured reading aids that can help, some are book markers with lines to help the reader stay online. Some are coloured tracking rulers to help with math and geometry.

Screen filters can be bought for computers, monitors and handheld devices. The screen filters can reduce glare and be bought in a variety of colours.

Paper, workbooks, printing paper and writing paper can also be bought in variety of colours that will help the most.

Appendix 6
Autistic brain processing model

Autism brain research can be confusing when it only highlights certain brain areas. Therefore, the reason for including this model and the associated brain parts is to help the reader understand how each individual brain part is involved in wider cognition for autism should they wish to further read about autism brain research.

The model goes through basic steps of brain function. It starts with sensory inputs and finishes off explaining behavioural motor output.

Figure 26: Autistic brain processing model and associated brain parts.

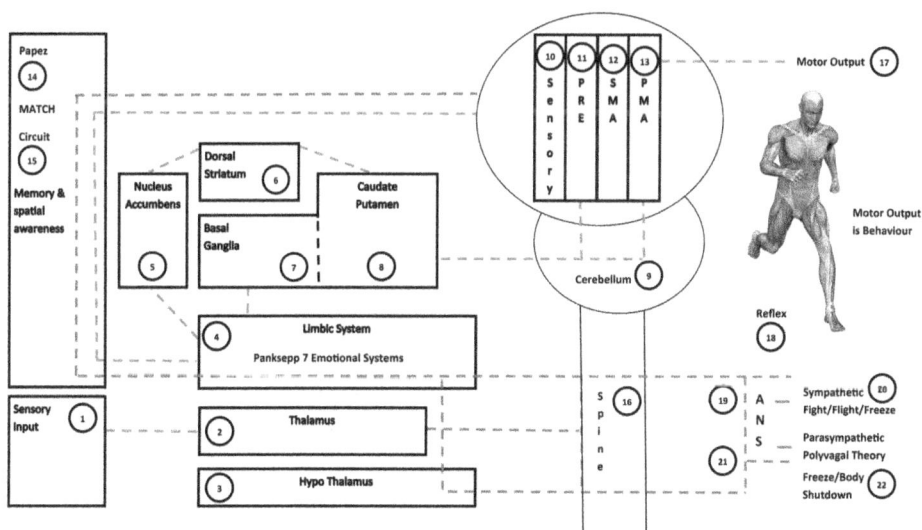

1	Sensory input	All sensory information is initially sent to the thalamus apart from smell, as smell has direct connections to the wider brain parts.
2	Thalamus	Helps relay sensory and motor information to other areas of the brain for wider sensory integration.
3	Hypothalamus	Helps keep homeostasis by supporting the autonomic nervous system. Supports regulation of eating, drinking, body temperature, stress and energy levels.
4	Limbic system	Is a set of structures that help process and regulate emotions and memory.
5	Nucleus Accumbens	Plays a central role in the reward circuit with mainly dopamine (promotes good feelings), and serotonin (promotes satiation).
6	Dorsal Striatum	Is involved with decision-making through the integration of sensorimotor, cognitive, emotional and motivational goal-oriented information.
7	Basal Ganglia	Responsible primarily for motor control. It also plays a role with motor learning, executive functioning and emotional regulation.
8	Cuadate Putamen	Helps regulate movements and influence various types of learning.
9	Cerebellum	Receives information from the sensory systems, the spinal cord, and other parts of the brain and then helps regulate motor movements. The cerebellum coordinates smooth voluntary movements such as posture, balance, coordination, and speech.
10	Sensory motor area	This area helps the brain perceives the sensation of sensory input both internally and externally. It helps the brain understand what areas and muscles are involved within certain sensory stimulation and motor action.
11	Premotor area	Is involved in planning and organising movements and actions.
12	Somatic sensory area	Is responsible for processing somatic sensations. These sensations arise from receptors positioned throughout the body.
13	Primary motor area	Controls voluntary movements needed for executive functioning skills.
14	Papez MATCH circuit	Plays an important role in the memory recall. It is a central pathway of the limbic system. If the executive function area of the brain is unsure what to do when faced with a problem, the Papez MATCH circuitry will retrieve any information from memory (spatial awareness and episodic memory) that is similar to problem as the memory may help the executive function area develop new ideas to overcome the problem.
15	Memory and spatial awareness	Is a cognitive process that enables a person to remember different locations as well as spatial relations of objects.
16	Spine reflexes	Usually a startle response to immediate threat.

17	Motor output	Movement of muscles through the pooling of motor neurons.
18	Reflex of muscles	Movement of muscles through the pooling of motor neurons.
19	Autonomic nervous responses	Acts largely unconsciously and regulates bodily functions. This system is the primarily in control of the fight or flight response.
20	Sympathetic nervous system (SNS): Fight and flight	When the body is stressed, the SNS contributes to what is known as part of the fight or flight response. The body shifts its energy resources toward fighting or fleeing from a threat. The SNS signals the adrenal glands to release hormones called adrenalin (epinephrine) and cortisol to help deal with the threat.
21	Parasympathetic nervous system	Sometimes called the rest and digest system. The parasympathetic system conserves energy as it slows the heart rate, increases intestinal and gland activity, and relaxes sphincter muscles in the gastrointestinal tract.
22	Parasympathetic nervous Freeze/ shutdown	If the parasympathetic system is activated intensely it could result in the person becoming immobilised. This is often referred to as the freeze response. Such experiences can result in fainting, catatonia and situational mutism.

Appendix 7
Microbiome, gut health explained

There is a high prevalence of autistic people that have problems with gut health. This appendix is to help people develop a wider understanding of what gut health is.

Humans need food from the external environment to stay alive. The energy from food and liquids provides all the nutrients the body needs. The breakdown of nutrients happens within the gastrointestinal tract, also known as the gut.

Good gut health helps the immune system stay healthy. If the gut is not functioning well the person can experience autoimmune difficulties and poor health.

The immune system and bacteria

Nutrition passes through the gut as this helps absorb the nutrients needed for overall health. However, such a process can result in problems as there are many harmful things in the external environment which can cause poor health if entered into the body through the gut. This is partly why humans have an immune system. The immune system is designed to spot these harmful foreign bodies, neutralise and destroy them before they negatively impact on health. This is why the immune system keeps the gut safe. The gut needs to function well enough to keep taking nutrients from food to keep the body alive. Also, healthy nutrition keeps the immune system functioning optimally.

Over time immune cells stores knowledge of potential threats which enables the wider immune system to produce antibodies and pathogen-fighting agents to keep the person healthy should they ever be exposed to a similar threat in the future. This is called natural immunity. This is why healthy exposure to the external environment during early development helps the immune system develop resilience needed for later life.

The vast majority of the immune system (about 80%) is located in the gut wall acting as a protective barrier preventing foreign bodies and pathogens from entering into the blood stream.

How food moves through the gut

There are two approaches to understanding how the gut works: the mechanical, and secondly through the function of bacteria.

The mechanical approach to understanding gut health

The digestive system has various components. First, there's the gastrointestinal tract which starts at the mouth and ends at the anus.

When anticipating food, glands within the mouth will start to produce saliva. Saliva and chewing change the food into a moist substance called bolus. The bolus then enters the oesophagus on its way to the stomach.

Nerves in the oesophagus will then start muscle contractions to help move the bolus along to the stomach. Once in the stomach the bolus is further broken down by being exposed to acids and enzymes that break down proteins. This process informs the pancreas, gallbladder and liver to produce digestive juices and bile for the duodenum for the next process of digestion.

After a while the bolus is altered into a liquid called chyme which is then sent to the small intestine. The liver sends bile to the gallbladder, which then delivers it to the duodenum which is located in the small intestine. Here, it dissolves the fats within the chyme so it can be easily digested. These enzyme-rich juices break the fat molecules down into fatty acids and glycerol which makes it easy for the body to absorb.

The enzymes also break down proteins into amino acids, and carbohydrates into glucose. This happens in the small intestine's lower regions, the jejunum and ileum which are coated in millions of tiny things called villi.

The villi create a huge surface area as this helps absorb amino acids, simple sugars, fatty acids and glycerol into the blood stream. The blood takes them to where they are needed throughout the body for overall function and health.

Leftover fibre, water and dead cells are then moved into the large intestine, also known as the colon. The body drains out most of the remaining fluid through the intestinal wall. What's left is a soft mass called stool, eventually passing through the anus.

The function of bacteria

A healthy gut contains immune cells, healthy bacteria and opportunistic bacteria all working together to both absorb nutrition and fight off infections and viruses. The accumulation of immune cells, healthy and opportunistic bacteria within the gut is called the microbiome.

Is the bacteria in the gut a bad thing? No, a healthy adult gut can carry up to 2kg of bacteria.

Different types of bacteria are needed to break down nutrition. Without such bacteria people would not survive. When bacteria do their job in the gut people are generally healthy.

Each person will have a different proportion of different types of bacteria in their gut which can be explained by genetics, environment, lifestyle and diet. Each person's bacterial system will be different; everyone has their own unique microbiome (make up of bacteria in the gut). Someone with a healthy balanced diet will likely have more biodiversity (more variation of gut bacteria) in their gut which results in better health compared with people who have a limited poor diet (limited variation of gut bacteria).

For simplicity, there are three types of bacteria in the gut which are collectively called gut flora. These are:

1. Beneficial flora
2. Opportunistic flora
3. Transitional flora

Beneficial flora bacteria

The beneficial flora bacteria are good bacteria as they act like the safeguards of the gut. They help digest foods and turn it into energy for the body to absorb. The good bacteria also keep the harmful bacteria in check which helps reduce inflammation and disease. Good bacteria help against bad bacteria such as candida (fungal infection caused by yeast), clostridium perfringens (food poisoning), campylobacter (from raw, uncooked food), listeria (contaminated foods) and various others such as norovirus and salmonella.

The good bacteria regulate the opportunistic flora (discussed in more detail later). Opportunistic flora seeks and destroys. This can be helpful in small doses to fight off unwanted pathogens, viruses and harmful bacteria. However, if opportunistic bacteria are left unchecked by the good bacteria it will start destroying healthy cells which may result in poor autoimmune health.

The balance of good and opportunistic bacteria for optimal health is 8:2. That is eight good bacteria to two opportunistic bacteria. A poor diet will upset this ratio of good and opportunistic bacteria. When this happens the opportunistic flora gets out of control and causes damage which prevents the good bacteria from doing its job effectively.

There are foods that help good bacteria. These are both prebiotics and probiotics.

- Prebiotics helps develop good bacteria.
- Probiotics is actual bacteria of certain types of food.

Prebiotics are substances which come mostly from fibre. Examples of prebiotics are onions, leeks, radishes. carrots, coconut, meat, seeds, tomatoes, bananas, garlic, chicory, dandelion greens and asparagus. The good bacteria (beneficial flora) eat the fibre. This helps ensure there is plenty of the good bacteria and this keeps the 8:2 ratio. If the good bacteria can't feed on fibre, say because of a poor diet, the 8:2 ratio diminishes and this unfortunately affords opportunistic flora to grow which results in poor gut and autoimmune health.

Probiotics are essentially foods that already have significant amounts of beneficial flora bacteria (the good bacteria). Examples of probiotics are pickled vegetables, vegetables, kimchi, sauerkraut and dairy products such as yogurt, kefir and buttermilk. A diet with plenty of probiotics helps ensure the ratio of good and bad bacteria stays within the 8:2 range.

Opportunistic flora bacteria

Opportunistic flora bacteria are labelled opportunistic for a reason. If this bacterium is left unchecked by the beneficial flora (the good bacteria from pre and probiotics) they start taking opportunities to perform other functions that are not healthy. This then interferes with gut resulting in poor autoimmune health.

Pathogens are organisms that cause disease. Examples of pathogens include viruses and fungi. The body can usually fight back against pathogens but only if there are enough good bacteria. Pathogens often cause problems when the immune system is weakened. Pathogens, including opportunistic bacteria, wear down the intestinal lining of the gut wall (enterocytes), therefore creating a leaky gut (gut dysbiosis). Having escaped the internal intestinal lining, the pathogens now enter the blood stream as antigens. This is when they create autoimmune difficulties as they attack cells and can possibly break through the blood barrier. The person then suffers from poor health and autoimmune problems.

Transitional flora bacteria

These are different types of microbes that we swallow every day in the foods and liquids we consume. When the gut is well-protected by the beneficial bacteria, this group of flora passes through our digestive tract without harming us. But when the beneficial flora is damaged and not working properly, transitional flora can cause diseases.

The modern diet is becoming more and more reliant on processed nutrition. Processed foods and liquids are usually pre-cooked, pre-packaged, canned and tinned. They all have an unnatural long shelf life compared with fresh food and liquids. In order to enable the long shelf-life, processed foods are usually coated in chemical microbes. These chemical microbes are designed to kill bacteria as this is what helps preserve the food to ensure the long shelf life. It is therefore obvious that the bacteria-killing chemical microbes found on processed foods, when consumed, will kill some of the good beneficial flora bacteria which will upset the 8:2 ratio of good and bad bacteria.

When the gut is well protected with a high ratio of beneficial flora bacteria, transitional flora and bacteria killing microbes go through the digestive tract without doing much harm. However, if the ratio is not high, transitional flora and bacteria killing microbes affords bad bacteria, viruses and pathogens to wreak havoc in the immune system resulting in poor health and disease, all of which will negatively impact on the biochemical pathways associated with autism.

Villus and enterocytes

The protective system that covers the intestines is called villi.

The epithelial cells (sometimes called enterocytes) coat the villi and are the very cells that complete the digestive process and absorb nutrients from food. These cells work very hard and therefore have to be constantly replaced. Enterocytes are constantly produced in the villa, slowly traveling to the top to replace the worn-out enterocytes that have previously did their job. This way the layer of the intestines gets constantly renewed to be as effective as it possibly can be for absorbing nutrients. Poor gut health hinders the renewal of enterocytes which can result in a leaky gut. The issue of a leaky gut can help explain allergies and intolerances for things such as gluten and grains.

Leaky Gut Syndrome (intestinal permeability)

A leaky gut is when the lining of the gut wall is damaged. The damage results in small gaps along parts of the lining. Harmful substances like pathogens, bad bacteria, gluten and small food particles can pass through these small holes, hence the name leaky gut. When harmful substances pass through these gaps they can cause all sorts of problems such as allergies, disease and poor autoimmune health.

There are many causes of a leaky gut. For example, a poor ratio of good and bad bacteria, poor diet, too many processed foods, prolonged stress, excess alcohol, medication and drug use can all result in a leaky gut.

Allergies and Intolerances

A potential source of allergies can frequently start in the digestive process of the small intestine. If the body fails to break down proteins into amino acids parts of protein molecules will remain. Under normal circumstances these proteins don't make it into the bloodstream. However, tiny particles can enter the lymphatic system through fat droplets, and once there, they can attract the attention of immune cells. When these immune cells discover these tiny particles they attack it as a foreign body even though it is only a part of a protein. For example, a rogue protein particle of a nut could eventually result in a nut allergy.

The immune response treats this tiny particle (for example the protein of a nut) as a foreign body because it should not have entered into the system at that point. The immune system then starts to treat all similar particles as a foreign body, so the next time they encounter it they are likely to attack it, hence the start of an intolerance and potential allergy. This explanation does not only apply to nuts, but it also applies to allergies caused by foods that are both fatty and rich in proteins such as milk, eggs and various others.

Gluten

For some people gluten can pass between cells of their gut wall in an undigested state. Unfortunately, this slackens the connections between the individual cells of the gut wall. This allows gluten and wheat proteins to enter areas they shouldn't be, and this raises an alarm in the immune system. One percent of the population has a genetic intolerance to gluten (coeliac disease), but a considerable higher number of people suffer from gluten sensitivity.

People with coeliac disease can suffer serious infections or damage to the villi of the gut wall if they continue to eat wheat which will result in a leaky gut. The most effective treatment for coeliac disease is a gluten free diet.

Gluten sensitivity is a very different condition compared to coeliac disease. Those with gluten sensitivity can eat small amounts of wheat without risking serious damage to their gut wall.

As already explained, the gut can become leaky for a short time through activities of severe stress, heavy bouts of drinking and a serious course of antibiotics. Sensitivity to gluten resulting from these temporary causes can sometimes look the same as the symptoms of coeliac disease.

Lactose

Lactose intolerance is a deficiency, not an allergy. It results from a failure to break down certain nutrients of lactose into smaller parts. Lactose is found in milk and milk dairy products. Lactose is a two-sugar molecule that is linked by chemical bonds. The body requires a digestive enzyme (lactase) to break that bond.

Lactase breaks down lactose within the gut for it to be absorbed. If the enzyme is missing similar problems arise to those caused by gluten sensitivity. The undigested lactose particles move into the large intestine where they become food for the gas-producing bacteria. This causes symptoms such as belly ache, diarrhoea and flatulence.

For 75% of the world's population, the gene for digesting lactose slowly begins to switch off as they get older. Lactose intolerance does not mean cutting out milk products altogether. People who have lactose intolerance still have enough lactose-splitting enzymes in their gut to consume small amounts of milky products.

Fructose

Fructose intolerance can be the result of a severe inability to metabolise fruit sugar. Such intolerance causes the digestive system to overreact to small amounts.

Other people affected by fructose intolerance actually have a condition more accurately described as fructose malabsorption and experience problems when exposed to larger amounts of fructose. Processed foods are often high in fructose.

The cells of people with fructose intolerance contain fewer fructose-processing enzymes. This naturally results in higher levels of unprocessed fructose left in the gut, which means this extra fructose will likely interfere with other gut processes.

Fructose intolerance that develops later in life is thought to be caused by a reduced ability for the gut to absorb fruit sugars. Such people often have fewer transporters (called GLUT-5 transporters) within their gut wall. When they ingest even a small amount of fruit sugar their limited transporters are overwhelmed, and the excess fructose ends up feeding the opportunistic flora (the bad bacteria).

Sugar helps the body absorb many other nutrients into the bloodstream. For example, the amino acid tryptophan uses fructose for digestion. Tryptophan is needed by the body to produce serotonin, the neurotransmitter needed for major neurological functions. The body can only absorb so much sugar into the bloodstream before it ultimately has to let excess sugar within the gut go to waste. However, as tryptophan has already combined to excess sugar, when the body gets rid of excess sugar it also loses much needed tryptophan.

The brain and gut connection: The vagal nerve

The main nerve connecting the gut and the brain is the vagus nerve (also called the vagal or polyvagal nerve). This nerve is the fastest and most important route from the gut to the brain.

Figure 14: Human Social Engagement System

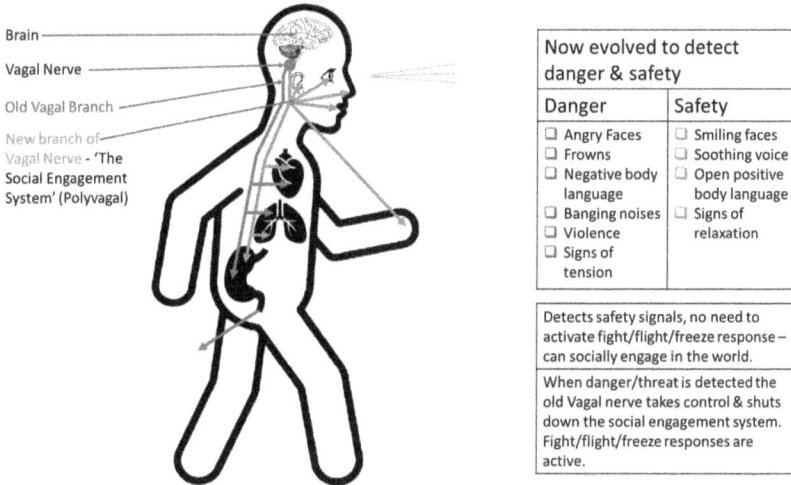

Now evolved to detect danger & safety	
Danger	Safety
☐ Angry Faces ☐ Frowns ☐ Negative body language ☐ Banging noises ☐ Violence ☐ Signs of tension	☐ Smiling faces ☐ Soothing voice ☐ Open positive body language ☐ Signs of relaxation

Detects safety signals, no need to activate fight/flight/freeze response – can socially engage in the world.
When danger/threat is detected the old Vagal nerve takes control & shuts down the social engagement system. Fight/flight/freeze responses are active.

Labels on figure: Brain; Vagal Nerve; Old Vagal Branch; New branch of Vagal Nerve - 'The Social Engagement System' (Polyvagal)

The vagus nerve picks up information from the body (lungs, gut and heart) and sends it to the brain. This helps the brain understand homeostasis as well as the general health of the gut.

Cooperation between the gut and brain begins very early in life. For example, the pleasant feeling of a full stomach or being upset when hungry or annoyed with wind is communicated through the vagus nerve.

When the brain senses potential danger it naturally wants to ensure safety. To do so, it needs energy to either fight or run away; the brain borrows energy from the gut to do so. The reason for this is because if there is danger in the environment it is better to stop digestion and gut processes for a short period so all available resources can help overcome a potential threat within the environment. The extra energy is then used to help aid the fight, flight and freeze responses. Interruption of gut processes results in symptoms of needing to go to the toilet.

The problem for people in modern society is that the alarm signals their ancestors used to detect danger is the same system used to detect abstract danger today. Such abstracted danger could be strangers, public speaking and various elements of social interactions. For example, an aggressive person, a frowning face, someone with a loud voice and people with negative body language can all trigger the ancient alarm signal which will interrupt gut processes.

In relation to autistic people, the difficulty in understanding neurotypical social interactions, sensory sensitivities and atypical executive function skills will often trigger the fight, flight or freeze responses on a daily basis.

If the gut has to continue to slow or stop gut processes due to the brain's perception of danger, then the gut microbiome will eventually suffer. The constant interruption of gut processes will negatively impact immune health. This may limit the function of beneficial flora (good bacteria), meaning opportunistic flora will start to cause havoc resulting in an unhealthier microbiome and poor autoimmune health for autistic people.

The microbiome needs good sources of B vitamins, particularly B6, B9 and B12. Without these vitamins it is likely the person will experience poor gut and autoimmune health.

Appendix 8
A bit about PDA

Most people seem to agree that pathological demand avoidance (PDA) is considered under the umbrella term of autistic spectrum. However, there are some differences between autism and PDA:

	Demand avoidance characteristics	Typical Autism
1. Resisting demands obsessively	Has good social and cognitive skills in avoiding demands, could even be described as influential or manipulative. Such skills could distract others, suggesting alternatives, elaborate excuses, withdrawing into fantasy and playful explanations for avoidance, or even outright rejection of perceived demand. Can be strategic when avoiding perceived demands. For example, different strategies may be used for different people.	Is usually reluctant to perceived demands. Often shuts out pressure in a non-social way. Has very limited conscious strategies for avoidance. Doesn't adapt a particular strategy for a particular person. Doesn't use social insight or manipulation to avoid perceived demands. For example, they are very direct, not socially strategic.
2. Appears very sociable on surface, but struggles with depth of social meaning	Can appear sociable but struggles with depth of social meaning. Often feel rules don't apply to them. Despite social awareness, behaviour is uninhibited: extreme giggling or inappropriate laughter. Children prefer adults compared to peers. Appearance can be "not that she can't but more she he won't". Praise and reward or often ineffective.	Can often struggle socially, often seek out rules to avoid the anxiety of the unknown.

3. Impulsivity, mood swings, switching suddenly	Can experience sudden mood swings or reactions to a perceived demand or pressure. Activity must be on the person's terms, can change mind in an instant if suspects someone else is in control.	Rarely impulsive, often transitioning to change slowly. Rules, structure, routine and predictability help.
4. Comfortable in role and pretend play, sometimes to an extreme	Very comfortable in role play and pretend play, sometimes to an extreme. May take over these roles when socially interacting as to avoid perceived demands. May imitate other authoritative figures to try and influence authority. For example, pretend they are a teacher, the boss or a famous person to exert control.	Can experience difficulty to sustain imitation over different social settings.
5. Language	Social timing is good except when interrupted. Social mimicry common. Repetitive questions used for distraction but may signal panic.	Too varied across the spectrum to determine pattern.
6. Obsessive behaviour, often focused on people rather than things	Obsessions can be of a social nature, such as people and generalised character traits.	Autistic people are generally more pre-occupied with things rather than people.

The obvious difference between PDA and autism is the PDA person is more capable of creating elaborate avoidance strategies in relation to perceived demands, often with elements of social fantasy. Instead, the autistic person would just avoid or workaround perceived demands. It is because of these differences that some people prefer to use the phrase pathological demand avoidant (PDA) instead of autism. However, it is generally agreed that there is much overlap between PDA and autism and that is why some people prefer PDA under the umbrella term of autism spectrum.

There could be two possible explanations to explain the difference between PDA and autism.

1. Atypical social development
2. Reactance theory.

Atypical play development

Just like autistic children, PDA children will have atypical social development. However, it may be that PDA children have mastered some elements of play during critical periods of early development.

Although they may have mastered some elements of play, they may still have some of the challenges associated with autism. For example, trying to understand how neurotypical people will behave and act, how social interactions will unfold and difficulties with some elements of problem-solving. Such challenges can cause significant stress for the PDA person, especially when demands are placed upon them. One coping strategy some PDA people use is to create fantasy tales to escape the demands placed on them.

If the PDA person has developed some elements of play skills during critical periods of development, this may help them engage in fantasy storytelling to avoid demands.

Play can create a world that is governed by fantasy, it is the experimentation of trying to develop a narrative of how to act. Having rehearsed stories about how people should act and behave in the world can be really helpful when faced with uncertainty. If the right hemisphere for the PDA person is having difficulty seeing the wider context it may rely on the left hemispheres narrowed understanding to have some sort of control, for example, already pre-rehearsed fantasy narratives that help avoid demands. That being said, not all PDA people will engage in social fantasy narratives.

Reactance theory

Reactance theory explains why some people (the general population) may experience a negative emotional reaction when exposed to rules, regulations, expectations, social demands and even sometimes consumer advertising.

Reactance theory explains that such expectations, or demands, threatens or reduces one's own perceived behavioural freedoms. The negative reactance occurs when a person feels that someone or something is taking away their freedom of choice and freewill. This is especially true for some people when the demand is mundane as it reduces the person's liberty and options to do other pleasant things.

Not always, but usually, the people who experience reactance have a creative personality. This makes sense; their personality traits push for exciting creative endeavours. The brain is motivated to do new things, explore different ideas, so it is natural for the brain to have a reactance to mundane boring tasks.

Reactance can occur when someone is heavily pressured to act in a certain prescribed way. Reactance can cause the person to avoid doing what is expected.

Could it be that people who are diagnosed with a PDA profile have mastered some elements of social imagination during early development, and this coupled with the character trait of reactance theory is what gives rise to the disposition known as PDA?

How to support reactance of any kind ... including PDA

The best strategy for people who have any reactance behaviour is to tell them, *"You don't have to, but..."* and then suggest what may need done. A person with PDA can even do this themselves, *"You can try doing x, but can always stop if you want to."* It seems by giving the person the option of opting out reduces the reactance and actually frees up the person to do the things they've been avoiding.

Other support strategies for PDA support

Avoid a firm or authoritative nature, statements or attitude. Instead, try and create a jovial atmosphere that respects the person.

Humour can help when you know what the person liked and finds humours. Take the time to understand what is interesting for the person.

Always frame demands or choices as if it is the person who is in control, use indirect statements when possible. For example:

- *"What would you say is best?"* Then present the only options the person has.
- *"I wonder what happens next?"* Even though you know the natural flow of things, the person may feel in control if given the impression it was their idea.
- *"I don't know how to do..."*. Is a good technique to get the person engaged by getting them to take the initiative.
- *"I bet you couldn't do ... I bet this can't be done in this amount of time ... I wonder who could do this fast?"* Reverse psychology can work.
- *"You don't have to if you don't want to"*. Is often a good way of making the person feel in control.
- Avoid any negative statements like *"This must happen now... you need to... you can't... you must do..."*

Appendix 9
Autism and LGBTQ

There is a higher prevalence of LGBTQ people within the autistic population. There are various theories as to why this is the case.

If the brain develops atypically, as we know it does for autistic people, then it is possible for the brain to experience a different gender compared to the sex of the body. This is because the sex of the body and the gender of the brain develop independently of each other; both having independent critical periods of development. For example, sex hormones that determine sex organisation of the body are different from the hormones that help sexualise the gender of the brain [1]. This can mean a person can be born with a typical female body but a male brain, or a male body and a female brain and everything else in between. Such diversity can possibly explain bisexuality, homosexuality and fluid gender identity. Although there is no strong empirical data to make such claims, there is some data that would suggest that the majority of LGBTQ individuals would fall into categories where brain and bodily sexuality don't match up [1]. However, it is clear biology has profound impact on sexual identity. For example, female typical brains are strongest for the majority of biological females, and male typical brains are strongest for the majority of biological males [1].

Around half of fertilised eggs have two X chromosomes, the other half are Y chromosomes. The determination of the biology of sex is determined by the eventual arrival of the sperm chromosome. The sperm chromosome will be either X or Y, which will result in the egg being either female (XX), or male (XY). Unless interrupted the default pathway for the developing foetus is to develop as female. Somewhere between six and twelve weeks of the pregnancy if the sperm is X the pregnancy will continue developing as female. If the sperm is male the Y chromosome triggers the gonads to secrete testosterone. The testosterone tells the brain to be male and this signals the development of a penis and testicles.

The *brain* is masculinised in boys by testosterone. For example, the Y chromosome promotes the growth of testicles which helps secrete testosterone. The brain is then masculinised when testosterone is converted to estrogen by an enzyme called aromatase.

Alternatively, the *body* is masculinised in boys when testosterone is to be converted into dihydrotestosterone (DHT) by an enzyme called 5-alpha-reductse [1].

If there is interruption during early gestation periods then the development of the baby will default back to female brain development. This can happen even though the physical body is male. This can explain why a male can be attracted towards another male, or why a male can be attracted to both females and males, or why a male may feel like a female, or a male who feels like male but in some aspects has female traits, and everything in between. This means interruption of early gestation periods may result in gender and sex differences, including a variation of GBTQ dispositions.

The entire B vitamin complex (B1, B2, B3, B5, B6, B7, B9, and B12) each have a role in testosterone and oestrogen regulation, particularly B3, B6 and B12. Developmental processes during the second trimester of gestation seem crucial in establishing the sexual identity of the human brain. As discussed in chapter 2, the biological surge of demand during pregnancy will mean between 19-29% of all pregnant mothers will be deficient in B vitamins, with the highest deficiency of B vitamins seen in the second trimester which could interrupt the brain gender development [2, 3].

Progesterone levels, along with estrogen and oxytocin are high through pregnancy but progesterone plummets close to labour.

B vitamins (particularly B6) also play an important role in the creation and activation of oestrogen and progesterone. Low levels of B vitamins can lead to reduced levels of oestrogen, again further impacting on things such as progesterone. The evidence is limited on how hormonal difference causes higher prevalence's for bisexuality in females, but there is consensus that hormonal difference during pregnancy does contribute to higher bisexuality in later female life. The early surge of estrogen is critical for masculinising the female brain. If the estrogen cannot be regulated (as in too much estrogen), then the physical female brain could be born with male typical attitudes [1]. This can explain why a female can be attracted towards another female, or why a female can be attracted to both females and males, or why a female may feel like a male, or a female who feels like female but in some aspects has male traits, and everything in between.

For the male foetus, if testosterone could not be converted to estrogen then he would be born with a feminised brain. It is therefore likely that atypical estrogen and testosterone levels during pregnancy could determine the maleness or femaleness of the brain. The impact on hormonal development of both testosterone, oestrogen and progesterone as a result of low B vitamins can start to explain why there may be a higher prevalence of LGBTQ dispositions within the autistic population.

As well as a possible biological explanation for higher LGBTQ prevalence's there may be a psychosocial contributing factor. Autistic people have often experienced being marginalised, ridiculed and bullied during their formative and adolescent years. Being marginalised and cast from the neurotypical social group can, for some people, cause internal conflict. Often autistic people question their identity with questions like *Who am I? Why don't I fit in? What is different about me? Why do people treat me differently?*

It has been well documented that such experiences for autistic people, especially during their formative and adolescent years, has led them to question if they may actually be the wrong sex or gender because they didn't fit in socially. Atypical social development will mean some autistic people will learn social roles, identities and genders differently. The opportunity of play to imitate and embody different genders, cultures and social roles has often been missed. This can partly explain why there may be a curiosity in later life about LGBTQ expression, especially if the persons biological development has been atypical during gestation.

Some autistic people may grow out of this stage, but others may start to experiment with their gender identity and expression, especially people with the personality trait for openness and creativity. This type of exploration and self-discovery leads itself towards the postmodern view of social construction of fluid gender identity and expression. As autistic people have often been marginalised, excluded and discriminated against by the majority of society, it is clear to see how autistic people often find liberty and freedom within the narrative of social construction.

There has been attempts throughout this book to explain there may be biological reasons why neurotypical people have developed such a neurotypical world. This is why society should not be explained solely through a postmodernist lens of social construction. It is likely these biological explanations can be traced to the neural play systems of play uncovered by Panksepp [4], which helps develop altruistic social reciprocity and social order. Alternatively, people also need to understand that there is also a high correlation between biology, LGBTQ and fluid gender identity. It is possible to explain LGBTQ and fluid gender identity through a social construction lens, but there is likely a biological basis that can also explain the diversity of gender and sex.

References

1. Panksepp, Jaak, et al. "Chapter 7." The Archaeology of Mind: Neuroevolutionary Origins of Human Emotions, W. W Norton, New York, 2012, pp. 267–275.
2. Prevalence of vitamin B-12 insufficiency during pregnancy and its effect on offspring birth weight: a systematic review and meta-analysis. Author: Sukumar, Nithya; Rafnsson, Snorri B. Publication: The American Journal of Clinical Nutrition. Publisher: Oxford University Press. Date: 2016-04-13
3. Ries, Julia. "Pregnant Women Aren't Getting Enough Nutrients." Healthline, Healthline Media, 24 June 2019, https://www.healthline.com/health-news/pregnant-women-arent-getting-the-vitamins-and-nutrients-they-need?msclkid=91a49710c15b11ec9fdf312770d44b13.

4. Panksepp, Jaak, et al. "Chapter 10." The Archaeology of Mind Neuroevolutionary Origins of Human Emotions, Norton, New York, N.Y, 2012.

A special thanks is needed to Lian, David, Liz, Joanna, Ian, George, Ruby, Scott, Amber and Bear.

www.ingramcontent.com/pod-product-compliance
Lightning Source LLC
Chambersburg PA
CBHW031431270326
41930CB00007B/656